PREACHING THE STORY

HOW TO COMMUNICATE GOD'S WORD THROUGH NARRATIVE SERMONS

JEFFREY W. FRYMIRE

Warner Press
ANDERSON, INDIANA

Coordinator of Communications and Publishing, Church of God Ministries, Inc.
PO Box 2420, Anderson, IN 46018-2420
800-848-2464 • www.chog.org

To purchase additional copies of this book, to inquire about distribution and for all other sales-related matters, please contact:

 Warner Press, Inc.
PO Box 2499, Anderson, IN 46018-9988
877-346-3974 • www.warnerpress.com

Cover and text design by Mary Jaracz

ISBN-13: 978-1-59317-131-5
ISBN-10: 1-59317-131-5

Library of Congress Cataloging-in-Publication Data

Frymire, Jeffrey W., 1953-
    Preaching the story : how to communicate God's Word through narrative sermons / by Jeffrey W. Frymire.
        p.   cm.
    Includes bibliographical references.
    ISBN-13: 978-1-59317-131-5 (pbk.) — ISBN-10: 1-59317-131-5 (pbk.)
    1. Narrative preaching. 2. Story sermons. 3. Preaching. I. Title.
BV4235.S76F79   2006
251—dc22   2006010594

Printed in the United States of America.
06 07 08 09 10 /EP/ 10 9 8 7 6 5 4 3 2 1

This book is dedicated to those who have helped me to preach the story:

To my parents, Frank and Florence, who told me my first stories and for whom, at their funerals, I had the privilege of telling their final stories;

To my in-laws, John, the finest pastor I have ever known, and Bertha, who even years after her passing remains my biggest fan;

To my mentor, Rev. Forrest Plants, who taught me to trust the storyteller that was in me and encouraged me to preach the story;

To giants of the pulpit—men like Dr. James Earl Massey, Dr. Samuel Hines, and President Robert Reardon—who spoke to my heart and soul as a young minister and invested in me the joyous and awesome charge to preach the Word;

To Rev. Horace Sheppard, Sr., who preached the story one night and offered to shake the hand of the first young person who would go to the altar and accept Jesus Christ as their Savior. That night he prayed over a seventeen-year-old boy at an altar and started my journey in Christ. More than four decades later, I still "feel constrained to say that I love this narrow way, singing glory, hallelujah, I'm one of them today";

But mostly, this book is dedicated to an incredible partner and friend who has loved me through good times and bad, through ups and downs, and through the fire and the rain and who has blessed me with three incredible children (Doug, Jonathan, and Joel, and their wives, Susan, Maria, and Shafali), who have given my life joy, meaning, and a wealth of stories that will take a lifetime to share.

CONTENTS

1

THE CHANGING FACE OF PREACHING
ON BEING THE LAST GENERATION

I love to tell the story! 'Twill be my theme in glory—
To tell the old, old story of Jesus and his love.

THE LAST GENERATION

We are the last generation to experience preaching in its current form. David Buttrick, the renowned homiletics author and professor, has said about the preaching scene, "The times they are a-changing."[1] Paul Scott Wilson is even more emphatic: "Not since the Middle Ages or the Reformation have such mighty winds swept the homiletical highlands."[2] Already the landscape of preaching is changing as technology moves the church forward. Congregations both small and large are riding the wave of video technology. Churches are now equipped with satellite dishes that bring the best and brightest church leaders to the sanctuary of congregations so small that they would never be able to either afford or host the crowds such leaders attract. By way

---

1. Buttrick, "On Doing Homiletics Today," 89.
2. Wilson, *Practice of Preaching*, 12.

of e-mail, these pastors and congregations can even interact with the leaders and ask questions concerning the subjects presented. With the advent of Internet access in most every church office and/or sanctuary, use of the resources provided by the Web have become so prevalent that sermons are infused with pictorial presentations rather than just verbal illustrations.[3]

I recently attended a church with fewer than 125 people in regular attendance. In spite of the relatively small size of the congregation, the pastor had filled the sermon with pictures of people, issues, and ideas that illustrated it. No longer content to merely tell the illustration, the pastor wanted the congregation to visually imagine the characters and individuals of whom he spoke.

Clips from movies now dot the preaching scene. Resources are available for using video sermon starters that can highlight a theme or conflict to introduce your sermon. People have dedicated whole books and Web sites to finding visual resources to aid in developing themes, ideas, and illustrations. I attended a large megachurch service and, along with the words to the songs and PowerPoint presentations, I saw the entire service projected on three large video screens hanging above the stage. The rounded video unit reminded me of the video scoreboard that you see at professional or college basketball arenas. Clearly, this isn't your grandfather's sermon presentation any more.

Undoubtedly, the changes occurring are not just technologically driven. The entire communication culture is changing all around us. These are profound and fundamental

---

3. Sites such as www.sermoncentral.com provide a Web-based sermon and sermon illustration resource and boast more than 70,000 resources available to assist preachers.

changes that will dominate the cultural landscape for generations to come. We have entered full blast into the information age. The influences of communications media on our culture are growing. We have moved from concern over the influence of TV to the megaindustry of movie production and video (DVD) distribution, which dominates our viewing habits. We can download material to our phones as we travel. Recently the preschool in the church where I pastor had a program for parents. Moms and dads stood up and gathered at the front of the auditorium when their son or daughter was singing. Each parent wanted to take a keepsake picture. More than half of them were taking pictures, not with cameras, but with their phones.

We have moved from having access to information on the Net as we sit at our office desk or at the home computer to an age where wireless technology is revolutionizing where and when we obtain our information. My wife and I went on sabbatical, and I took along my laptop with wireless network connectivity. I could access the Web in the car, at the fast-food outlet, or in my father-in-law's house (he has no wireless network, but someone in the neighborhood does). Most college campuses, cafés, hotels, and libraries have wireless networks you can access. Whole cities are going WiFi (high-speed wireless Internet). Current Analysis, a leading business information analysis group, reported that sales of laptop computers exceeded that of desktop computers for the first time in May 2005. The group reported that one of the main reasons for the change was that "more people require computers with WiFi or wireless capability...The demand is illustrated in the rise of notebooks that offer wireless. Last year, 80 percent of notebooks offered wireless; this year, it's 95 percent."[4] We are heading toward a day when Internet access will be available anywhere and everywhere without wires, much like the changes in phone technology have taken us from a kitchen phone to a cordless phone to cell phones. Not since Gutenberg and the invention of the moveable type (in the 1450s) have we experienced such a technological revolution in how we access information. It's entirely possible, if not probable, that the information above will seem unremarkable by the time you read this book and will be outdated by the time it comes from the printer.

Such changes are revolutionizing not only how and where we receive information, but also who is publishing the information we receive. During the 2004 presidential election, "blogs" (short for We*b logs,* online personal journals or logs) became the revolutionary new player in the business of information. "Before this year, blogs were a curiosity, a cult phenomenon, a faintly embarrassing hobby on the order of ham radio and stamp collecting. But in 2004, blogs unexpectedly vaulted into the pantheon of major media, alongside TV, radio, and, yes, magazines."[5] We no longer live merely in the information age; we also live in the *instant* information age.

THE CHANGING FACE OF WORSHIP

Music and worship have undergone similar changes. We have moved from piano and organ to electric guitars and synthesizers. A decade-long war in the church over styles of music has left us with no unified body of music and few distinguishing songs that are unique to the

---

4. As reported by the Associated Press in a *Times Daily* online edition of June 3, 2005.
5. Grossman, "Blogs Have Their Day," 109.

denomination or movement singing them. Worship de-emphasizes preaching in many churches. The key to building a successful congregation has become the singing, not the preaching. Now most congregations even make a distinction between singing and preaching, calling the first "worship" (as though worship can be defined by prayer, singing, specials, and an offering) and the second "preaching" (as though the proclamation of the Word can be limited to sermons, pulpits, and professional clergy).

The technological ramifications for preaching have become ever greater in other parts of the worship experience. Congregations have put computers in the sanctuary and are using Song Show Plus, Media Shout, and a variety of other programs to create visual accessories to the verbal content or worship. Denominational headquarters and parachurch organizations are producing videos for use in worship. I know of a church that gives out a DVD to their visitors instead of the usual packet of promotional materials or trinkets with the name of the church on them. The demise of Sunday evening worship has led to the rise in Saturday evening contemporary services. A few years ago, I was leading a conference where Walt Kallestad, pastor of Community Church of Joy in Phoenix, was one of the featured speakers. He told the group that Joy Church had numerous services on both Saturday and Sunday. One of the worship services had a country-and-western style of worship (Walt said he didn't preach at that one) while others ranged from ultracontemporary to orthodox Lutheran liturgy. He said that the later on Sunday one attends their church services, the more Lutheran the services became. Variety in style and music preferences in worship has become the norm.

Churches of all shapes and sizes have entered the theatrical age. Full-blown musical dramas during the holidays have replaced the choir cantatas of years past. Lights, special sound effects, live animals, two- and three-story sets, costumes, makeup, and stage design have come into the sanctuary. Megachurches like Southeast Christian Church in Louisville advertise their Easter pageant throughout the year, using it as a major way to attract visitors.[6]

With all that in mind, why are we still preaching in the same manner that we have for the last century? The only really noticeable change in preaching that has occurred during the last hundred years is that revivals went from two weeks to four days to rarely being seen. Camp meetings went from crowded ten-day events at campgrounds in the country to two- or three-day seminars in hotel convention centers. But over the last century, preaching has not fundamentally changed its approach. We remain wedded to the "three points and a cloud of dust" scenario for the preaching event. Propositional truths remain the dominant process by which we deal with texts of Scripture. Though we have healthy debates about the value and process of exegetical versus topical sermon styles, our basic approach remains the same. Haddon Robinson relates what happened when he was in a Bible study with business executives. The conversation turned to talking about how their pastor would feel out of place in their work/office environment. Eventually, they began evaluating their pastors' preaching, and they regarded it as being out of touch with the issues they face on an everyday basis. One of them said, "As much as I appreciate my

---

6. The church heavily features their pageant, *Living Hope*, on their Web site and in their visitor center. When I visited, it was May, so the Easter season had been over for nearly two months.

pastor and enjoy his sermons, it's not often that he speaks about my world."[7] Much of this has to do with our approach to a preaching methodology.

THE IMPORTANCE OF STORY

We live in a culture that is more affected by story than by technology (and we have already seen the effects of technology on our culture). The residual effects of watching TV have less to do with its use of too much violence and more to do with our raising multiple generations who are now enamored with story. For several years, my wife and I hosted a small group in our home called Hollywood and Theology. We watched numerous Hollywood-produced movies and then spent the next hour discussing the theological meaning of the movie. The premise of the group was that Hollywood has become the dominant teacher of theology to the masses in our age. While we learned much about popular culture and faith concepts from watching these movies, one evening stood out to me in particular. After spending several years watching movies that, in our view, either misrepresented Christianity or taught theological ideas contrary to biblical teachings, we finally watched a movie explicitly about redemption, salvation, and faith. It was an older movie recommended by a movie critic as positively portraying the Christian faith. The movie was *Tender Mercies* (1983), starring Robert Duvall. It was the movie for which he won the Oscar for Best Actor. The group, almost exclusively an under-forty crowd, was unanimously critical of the film—not for its theology, but for the holes in the story and the poor quality of the editing. For most of the discussion,

---

7. Hybels et al., *Mastering Contemporary Preaching*, 17–19.

the theology of the movie (which was why we were there) was secondary to the quality of the story. Clearly, this group cared deeply about the quality of the story and the presentation of that story.

One of the final movies we watched was *A Walk to Remember* (2002), starring Mandy Moore. The film follows the life of a devout Christian girl who eventually dates, falls in love with, and marries a young man who is anything but Christian. The story details his changing attitudes toward her faith, and it contains a remarkable conversion scene (remarkable for Hollywood, at least). Again, the discussion in our group centered on the story rather than its theological or biblical content. Our group didn't like the story, so they didn't like the movie. My conclusion? If you want to teach heresy, you can easily do so if you package it well and put it in a compelling story.[8] Conversely, if you teach Christian values and biblical truths and put it in the context of a poor story, you will get a limited audience and have a minimal impact. If you use a film to tell a compelling story in a powerful way and teach the story of Jesus with integrity and detail, you can confound the critics—just ask Mel Gibson and his movie phenomenon *The Passion of the Christ* (2004). Is the story we tell really that important? The people sitting around the TV that night were worship

---

8. This same group watched the original *Exorcist* movie (1973). This blockbuster film set out to teach moviegoers that God is so impotent that he cannot or will not protect a faithful priest who can, by faith and reliance on God, exorcise the demonic spirit. At the same time the hero, full of doubts and loss of faith, takes matters into his own hands and defeats the evil spirit by committing suicide and (supposedly) destroying the satanic presence. Clearly, this is not orthodox Christian doctrine. But it certainly was packaged in an engaging story, with visually gripping effects.

leaders, Sunday school teachers, small-group leaders, church board members, and devoted Christians. They were neither unconcerned nor ignorant about biblical things. But to them, story took precedence.

Maybe the best example of the importance of story in our video culture comes from the release of George Lucas's final installment of the blockbuster series Star Wars (1977–2005). If any movie changed the landscape of technology in film, it had to be the original *Star Wars* movie.[9] With the founding of Lucas's company, ILM (Industrial Light and Magic), the course of special effects took a dramatic turn and films now have a new threshold of computer-generated reality to live up to. But with the final release (*Star Wars: Episode III, Revenge of the Sith*), Lucas had a unique challenge. The public had already seen *Episode IV*, so moviegoers knew how the story of *Episode III* had to end. How could the producer create interest in a plot where the ending is a known commodity? After watching the movie (and yes, I was at a 12:01 AM showing with my wife, my two sons, and their fiancées), the discussion in our family and with everyone else centered, amazingly, on the story! If you liked the film, you didn't talk about Yoda's sword fighting or whether Ewen McGregor had aged enough to look like Alec Guinness (the original Obi-Wan Kenobi); you talked about the story. Did you like how the characters came to their respective ends? Did you think the transformation to Darth Vader worked? Did you expect the traitorous slaughter of the Jedi Knights, including the Padawan Learners? In spite of incredible technological special effects, groundbreaking science-fiction

---

9. People now refer to the original movie, *Star Wars*, by its full title, *Star Wars: Episode IV, A New Hope* or simply *Episode IV*.

worlds and characters, and six episodes of a story told in reverse trilogy order, the success of the movie depended on one aspect: was the story good enough to keep your attention?

Because the media culture around us has brought up multiple generations, we now view information not just as accumulated facts but as a progressive story. National and local news comes to us, not as the reporting of facts, but as the unveiling of story. Murder cases—from O. J. Simpson to Scott Peterson to the Marcus Wesson family mass murders—fascinate us because they unveil the stories of people's lives behind the scenes. The headlines suddenly reveal that O. J. is not the happy-go-lucky ex-football hero dashing through airports but a moody wife-beater capable of great violence. Scott Peterson is revealed as a clean-cut professional man leading a double life with his secret mistress, Amber Frye. Marcus Wesson had a family cult group that included not only his children with his wife but also children he fathered in an incestuous relationship with his daughters. The television and Internet play out their stories for all the generations to see, hear, and digest. Oprah Winfrey, Bill O'Reilly, and Jerry Springer are all popular media figures because they host story-driven shows that help us see the backgrounds of lives we know, wish we knew, are repulsed by, or are intrigued by. We are a story-driven culture.

Why, then, is our preaching not story-driven? If we have adapted other aspects of our daily lives and our worship experiences to changes in the culture, why does the style of our preaching remain mired in an old paradigm? One of the first rules I ever learned about paradigms is this: "Once there is a paradigm shift, everything goes back to zero."[10] The paradigm shift of the instant information age has taken

---

10. Barker, *Business of Paradigms*.

us from extrapolating a dry text to unveiling the incredible mystery of life through an unfolding story. This affects how we view the world around us, and the pulpit should reflect this change, especially since the great resource of the pulpit, the written Word of God, is the greatest storybook ever written. Let me illustrate.

THE POWER OF STORY

It was Easter, and we had just finished what one could graciously term a typical Easter service. In a small new church plant (less than fifty in average attendance), we didn't have a lot of options when it came to celebrating Easter Sunday. My wife had created a choir (less than ten people), and we had sung the songs of the resurrection. I had preached a sermon about Easter. I can't recall today what I preached about specifically, but it was an unremarkable sermon in terms of uniqueness or creativity. I know that it had stayed close to the gospel story of the resurrection of Christ. But it was not a sermon to revolutionize anyone's thinking about the power and mystery of the resurrection. After all, I had only told the story of the resurrection, and everyone knew the story. All I tried to do was apply it to the lives of the little group that called this gathering their home church.

Following the service, I was greeting people and wishing them a happy Easter. Janice, a young twenty-eight-year-old mother of two, approached me and said the most remarkable thing I had ever heard as a young pastor. Perhaps the statement was so startling to me because I was in my first pastorate, with preconceived notions about what the general population of the United States knew about spiritual things. I couldn't imagine anyone not knowing what she, apparently, didn't know. At any rate, her statement took me by surprise: "Pastor, thank you for the service today. You know, I never knew what Easter was really all about. I thought it was just a day about bunny rabbits, eggs, and candy. I didn't know it was about the resurrection of Jesus." Imagine not knowing the real story of Easter! Now, Janice was not a recluse. She did not have an out-of-the-ordinary social background. She was not religiously ignorant. Parents and pastor had raised and catechized her in a church. While she was reconnecting to her faith after many years of absence, her background was comparable to that of many young adults who have been exposed to religion but have not really participated in it. She knew who God was. She knew that Jesus was the Son of God. But she didn't know the story of the resurrection. I was dumbfounded. How could anyone grow up in twentieth-century America in a Christian church setting and not know the basic facts about Easter?

That day I made a decision that would profoundly affect the next twenty-five plus years of my preaching. I determined that I would spend more time telling stories than preaching sermons; I would preach more from the Gospels than I would from the Epistles; I would not leave Old Testament texts to use only on special occasions, but I would mine the depths of the stories of Moses, Joshua, David, Samuel, and others regularly. Since then, I have spent nearly one-third of my preaching years in the Gospels. I have preached through each one, and some of them twice. I have spent another third of my preaching years in the narratives of the Old Testament, which are so rich in stories about heroes of the faith. That Easter, I came to realize that the life of Jesus Christ and the stories told about him, the parable stories of Jesus, and the historical sections of the book of Acts and the Old Testament were far more powerful than I had ever imagined. And if you've read thus far, you probably do too.

JESUS AND THE EMPHASIS ON STORY

Jesus was a storyteller. Every time he spoke to crowds, he spoke in narrative. He told parables, used visual illustrations, commented on things he (and others) observed in the marketplace, in the field, or at worship. Jesus never apologized or backed away from the fact that, as a rabbi (a teacher), he was a teller of tales. This was hardly the case for the Jewish religious leaders. The Pharisees were far more serious. They spoke of the Law, mined the Torah for nuggets of moral truth, and told the crowd how the good Jew acted according to the oral law. But when Jesus spoke to the crowd, he appealed not to the facts of the Jewish Scriptures but to the heart of God's revelation in the Law and the Prophets and how that revelation appeared in everyday life. The Pharisees spent their days teaching small groups of zealous adherents preparing for induction into their Pharisaical society. Jesus roamed the countryside and backwater towns of Galilee and drew crowds in the thousands. And the crowds reacted with amazement at his teaching style and content. They were used to the didactic methodology of the Pharisees. Propositional truths shaped their normal teaching style: If you know this, then this is true. Jesus broke all the rules about teaching. In the process, he reached people's minds, hearts, and souls. As a result, the crowds of common people said that Jesus taught them as one who had authority (Matt 7:29). What was the authority with which he spoke? It was the power of story and the impact of storytelling. He made what had only been words on a scroll come alive in the minds and eyes of everyone to whom he spoke. To a generation of people who were largely illiterate or rarely read the written word, his ability to speak in pictures and connect to the events of their everyday lives carried with it the ring of divine authority. Jesus spoke the message that the Father had sent him to speak almost exclusively in story form.

He spoke to the crowd about the problems of inheriting when someone is the youngest rather than the oldest child (prodigal son story, Luke 15:11–32). He told of the common experience of losing something very valuable (lost coin, Luke 15:8–10). Jesus taught the crowd the real meaning of hospitality in a culture that already valued the idea of hospitality (good Samaritan, Luke 10:29–37). He talked about the trade he knew best when he told a parable about building a house (wise and foolish builders, Matt 7:24–27). He often spoke about the meaning of money and how to invest, spend, and give it away (workers in the vineyard, Matt 20:1–16; rich fool, Luke 12:13–21; talents, Matt 25:14–30; two debtors, Luke 7:36–50). He frequently spoke about caring for and breeding animals (the good shepherd, John 10:1–18; the lost sheep, Matt 18:10–14 and Luke 15:1–7; sheep and goats, Matt 25:31–46). He applied spiritual insights to the common everyday experience of farming (weeds, Matt 13:24–30; sower, Matt 13:1–9, 18–23; Mark 4:1–9, 13–20; and Luke 8:4–8, 11–15; new wine in old wineskins, Matt 9:17; Mark 2:22; Luke 5:37–39).

He taught them what it meant to be a change agent in society, not just by healing diseased and crippled bodies, but also by meeting common needs such as changing water into wine (Matt 2:1–11). and creating a smorgasbord from a boy's lunch pail (Matt 14:13–21; Mark 6:30–44; Luke 9:10–17; John 6:1–15). There even came a point in the ministry and preaching of Jesus when he decided that storytelling was such a powerful and effective tool that he would not teach the crowds without the use of parables. Matthew writes, "Jesus spoke all these things to the crowd in parables; he did not say anything to them without using a parable" (Matt 13:34).[11] Even when Matthew recorded the Sermon on the Mount, he preserved the pictures, stories, and images that encapsulated Jesus' teaching style. In this single sermon, Jesus spoke of salt and light, a city set on a hill, a lamp under a bushel basket, leaving the altar to be reconciled to your brother, being handed over to the judge, looking at a woman with lust, divorcing a wife, swearing oaths, taking revenge, and on and on. One is hard-pressed to say how today's preaching reflects Jesus' preaching style. Even when one boils down his common themes over three years of preaching, we still remember them as pictures and stories.

The dynamic power of Jesus' preaching was in the stories he told. This was no dry lecturer who stood up and extolled the intricacies of Jewish law. This was a preacher in the greatest sense of that word. He came to both inspire and teach, to challenge the conventions of the day, to think new thoughts and bring freshness to the dry bones of the Old Testament law. In the hands of Jesus, even the mundane listings of the books of Exodus, Leviticus, and Deuteronomy became visual pictures of turning the other cheek, walking the extra mile, or giving away your cloak as well as your tunic to one who would sue you for just one of them (Matt 5:39–41). These were not mere illustrations designed to explain the main point of his sermon. These *were* the main points of his sermon. They were his style. It was how he preached. It

---

11. What readers often overlook in that statement is that Matthew sees this as a fulfillment of Old Testament prophecy and quotes Psalm 78:2. In other words, Matthew expects that the Messiah would characteristically fulfill the psalmist's prophecy of speaking only in parables and, in doing so, would "utter things hidden since the creation of the world" (Matt 13:34; cf. Ps 78:2). I develop this concept more fully in chap. 5.

was how he taught with authority. It was his example to us, showing us how to preach and teach. Jesus was a storyteller.

ENTERING INTO THE LIFE OF THE STORY

What has become of Jesus' example? In the current state of preaching, the closest we come to teaching in parables and stories is making sure that we have illustrations in our sermons. Even then, we make sure we limit those stories to opening and closing illustrations. We treat the preaching task in our worship services as if it were a deliberative body like the U.S. Senate, where we can persuade others to believe as we do or to think about things as we think. We come dangerously close to crossing over the line and preaching like Pharisees or Sadducees (some would say we have already crossed the line or at least blurred it beyond distinction). We have exchanged the trade of storytelling for the process of prepared speeches. Have you ever had a visitor unaccustomed to hearing sermons try to compliment you on your preaching? I have. The compliment usually goes like this: "Pastor, that was a wonderful, uh, well, umm, talk you gave today. Good speech!" (If you haven't been raised in the church, you don't even know what to call what a preacher does!) I know few preachers who would call what they do a "speech" or a "talk"; it is supposed to be something much greater and much more intentional than a speech. James Earl Massey says, "A sermon is something more than a preacher's speech to his hearers; the sermon is also the preacher's response to what speaks livingly within him."[12] Yet, in our world today, the only thing that someone unfamiliar with a sermon can call it is just that—a speech.

---

12. Massey, *Responsible Pulpit*, 53.

Can you read the Sermon on the Mount and say, "Hey, nice speech"? Hardly. But why not? Because, at its heart, the Sermon on the Mount and most every other aspect of Jesus' revelation about God and of God's revelation of Jesus to the world is a story. And people want to hear stories told with detail and emotion, with power and movement. Give a person a speech to deliver, and it usually comes off as dry and stilted. Ask them to share a personal story or to tell about an event that they experienced, and their voice changes, their cadence increases, and their inflections become larger and more pronounced. We relate stories differently than speeches.

Lucille and Bren Breneman, in their excellent storytelling handbook, relate the story of one of their students who simply could not make the transition from monotone recitation to the art of storytelling. Despite several private sessions with the teachers, he was still not catching the concept. Suddenly, however, while telling a children's story in front of the whole class, something happened and he came alive. According to the Brenemans, "The boy was totally involved with the telling. No longer was he just relating incidents, he was personally living them. He had entered never-never land and taken us with him."[13] This is the power of story. You enter into the world of the story. "'Story' is a mystery that has the power to reach within each of us, to command emotion, to compel involvement, and to transport us into timelessness. 'Story' is a structural abstraction perhaps built into human memory, a way of thinking, a primary organizer of information and ideas, the soul of a culture, and the mythic and metaphoric consciousness of a people. It is a

---

13. Breneman and Breneman, *Once upon a Time*, 10.

prehistoric and historic thread of human awareness, a way in which we can know, remember, and understand."[14]

Entering into the world of story is essential to hermeneutical preparation. We must come to know the world of the biblical writer and of the story. We become immersed in the *Sitz im Leben*,[15] in the life of the event. The historical context becomes more than just background. It becomes the milieu in which the revelation of Scripture takes place. One cannot understand the book of Revelation unless one understands the political climate of the mid-first-century Roman world. Neither can a preacher properly exegete Isaiah without understanding that Isaiah is related to King Uzziah, his hero, and therefore he is part of the aristocracy of Israel (Isa 6:1; *b. Meg.* 10b). A preacher who doesn't know the first-century problems associated with Gnosticism will miss the dynamic of 1 John 1. Certainly, we will never fully appreciate the teachings of Jesus unless we know the world of smells, crop producing, and Talmudic laws that were an essential part of Jewish culture. This basic requirement of sermon preparation, entering into the world we are describing, places us on the cusp of being storytellers in our preaching. Without it, we are as lost as the young man in the Brenemans' class. When we learn to enter into the life of the biblical stories we preach, we can make the move from just reflecting on the passage of Scripture to drawing our hearers into the Word of God.

Just how you do this is the focus of the rest of this book. Read on—the story has just begun.

---

14. Livo and Rietz, *Storytelling*, 2.

15. This German term, meaning "situation in life" or "setting in life," is often used in describing the historical setting or, in form criticism, the sociological setting of the genre of literature being used in the Bible. I use it here in its broader sense of the life situation of the text.

2

TEXT AND CONTEXT
STEPPING-STONES TO STORYTELLING

I love the tell the story— 'tis pleasant to repeat
What seems, each time I tell it, more wonderfully sweet.

STEPPING-STONE 1
PREACHING *WHOLES* INSTEAD OF *HOLES*

While attending a preaching conference early in my ministry, the late Samuel Hines[1] challenged me to become a "series preacher." Dr. Hines was a master homiletician who had learned to mine the Scriptures for its depth and truth. He passionately spoke to pastors about the joys of preaching, especially preaching through an entire book of the Bible. One of his main points was that series preaching gave a congregation the whole story of a book. Some preachers cut up Scripture into small sections that seem not to be connected with one another—a typical practice in most preaching schedules, even those who take themes and create

---

1. Dr. Hines was the long-term pastor of the Third Street Church of God in Washington, DC, and was known all over the world for his masterful preaching and his exegetical style. I was privileged to sit under his guidance many times in both formal and informal settings.

a series based on a thematic idea. Instead, Dr. Hines argued that we should preach the "whole counsel of God" rather than just our favorite sections. He challenged us to turn our "holes into wholes." The argument seemed compelling to me, and that day I chose to become a series preacher.

One of the consequences of that decision is that by becoming a series preacher, I am much more conscious of Scripture as a whole than I would be if I were preaching short series based on themes. Dr. Hines always stressed the importance of placing a biblical text in the context of the chapter. He also encouraged us to find that context in the larger context of the book in which it appeared. Then, we were to find how the text fit into the whole book and how that whole book fit into its historical section of Scripture, into the Testament where found, and finally, into the Bible as a whole. That seemed to me to be a daunting task. After all, can't Romans 8:28 stand on its own? Must I find out how it relates to the paragraphs before and after it? Do I have to know how it fits into the chapter and section of Romans where found? Do I have to know how Paul's statement about God's love fits into the whole development of the first-century church's thought and writings? Do I need to know how this promise relates to the whole New Testament? Do I need to know how it relates to the Old Testament? Simply put, the answer is yes. God never places his Word into a context that causes it to be in conflict with other parts of his revelation. To do a proper hermeneutical study, I should know the full and complete biblical context and historical context of the text I am preaching. Most textbooks on preaching teach this basic philosophy.

However, most preaching today seems disconnected from the whole revelation of God. The popular trend is to take a concept or theme and break it down into about four or five sermons. Rick Warren's hugely successful book *The Purpose-Driven Life* is an example of such thematic study. Five purposes form the core of the book, and when a congregation does the forty-day journey based on the book, these themes also form the core of the preaching experience. My purpose here is not to criticize Rick Warren's book or teaching but only to point out that it represents the common segmented approach to preaching that is being done in the pulpit today. The idea is that by delivering a series of four or five sermons, the preacher can give an overview of a subject or idea that will be helpful for members of the congregation. Neither Warren nor any other responsible preacher would suggest that they could cover the depth of any biblical subject in just four or five sermons. The point of the study is not to exhaust a subject but to introduce it in sufficient depth that hearers can do two things: First, they can begin to appropriate the teaching into their lives. Second, they can delve into the subject in greater depth in personal or group study. However, such thematic sermons tend to disconnect the listener from the whole of scriptural revelation by breaking the story of Scripture down into "manageable bites." While this has some advantages, it trivializes the Bible and reduces the effectiveness of the sermons we preach. How? By creating in the minds of parishioners the thought that after four or five sermons, we have covered the subject!

The series preacher spends more time preaching longer series. For instance, one way to create an understanding of how Romans 8:28 fits into the larger context of the book of Romans would be to do a series on the whole book of Romans. By covering the paragraphs, sections, and chapters that both precede and follow 8:28, we put this important passage in the full context of the full book. People in the pew are able to hear and sense the fullness of Paul's theology and teaching by sitting under weekly teaching that takes into account the whole book of Romans. Last, it makes everyone (listener and speaker alike) sensitive to the story of why Paul wrote Romans and how that story impacts the writing of Paul and the letter's recipients in Rome. The preacher accomplishes all this by continually placing the sermon in the context of the whole.

Fred Craddock has described sermons as being either deductive or inductive. In deductive preaching, the preacher begins with a determined outcome. Craddock sees a deductive sermon as one in which "the conclusion precedes the development, a most unnatural mode of communication."[2] By its nature, deductive preaching (the most common form we hear today) treats the scriptural passage as a series of propositional truths rather than a revelation of the whole gospel. Inductive preaching, on the other hand, takes the opposite tack. An inductive preacher senses that the movement from application of a specific event to a much broader or more general application is the proper way to approach a scriptural passage. In other words, inductive preaching begins with a specific story or event and makes a more general application of the text to all of life. Craddock says that inductive preaching creates interest because "everyone lives inductively, not deductively."[3] In inductive preaching, one considers the reality of the whole story, the whole revelation, the whole text. The preacher moves from the story to the application, not from the application to the story.[4]

---

2. Craddock, *As One without Authority*, 1.

3. Ibid., 60.

4. For a more in-depth analysis of this, see Lowry's excellent treatment of Craddock's theories in Lowry, *Sermon*.

We dare not disconnect Scripture passages from the larger whole. Surely the first step toward preaching heresy is to disconnect this sermon and this passage from all of the revelation that God has given. If there is a case to be made for narrative preaching, it may be found in this very idea. Narrative preaching requires the preacher to view the passage in the context of the whole. Since narrative preaching requires us to understand the whole story in order to tell any of the story, in our sermon preparation, we must consider the full story rather than a selected text or theme. When we preach narratively, we make a statement about the importance of the whole Bible rather than just the part we read today.

For example, to tell the story of Elijah requires us to know how Jezebel influenced Ahab to become a Baal worshipper and how they both influenced the nation to abandon its historic faith in the Yahweh (Lord) God to follow a false god. It also requires us to understand the struggle and dynamic of a divided nation. How did it get that way? Elijah's sudden appearance on the scene makes us wonder what other prophets were doing during this time period. Certainly, preaching a narrative sermon on the story of Elijah requires us to understand how God is bringing about his plan in the midst of a rebellious nation that eventually he must destroy in order to save. We have to know how God's covenant with these people began, how they break it, and how the coming of Jesus Christ changes the covenant. All this is inherent in the text and becomes even more necessary when we begin to see the story as a part of the larger whole.

Dealing with the fullness of the biblical story will not only keep us cognizant of the whole revelation of Scripture; it also allows us to make a powerful statement about the importance and unity of the Bible. To preach narratively proclaims that you believe in the unity of Scripture and the whole revelation of Scripture from Genesis to Revelation. Joel Green makes this point quite well in the book *Narrative Reading, Narrative Preaching*:

> To speak of "the narrative of Scripture" is to make a theological claim that takes us beyond the warrants of any one of the books compromising the Bible, or even what might be strictly authorized by one or another of the Bible's Testaments. It is to insist that the whole of the Bible is, in Christian engagement, more than the sum of the parts, and that we can and should account for a theological presumption behind and woven into this collection of books. The particular contribution of the concept of "narrative" is the attribution to these books of a single, coordinating and unifying, plot. These words, these books, these collections of books, read as a whole, are said to generate a coherence that might otherwise be missing, or hidden, apart from the whole. For narrative, plot holds together and integrates into a single and complete whole what would otherwise be multiple and scattered.[5]

A pastor friend of mine used to start every sermon with the phrase "Last week we studied..." While I still believe this is not a very effective way to open a sermon, it did remind his congregation, What I am saying today is not disconnected from what we shared together last week in the previous passage, and it will not be removed from what we will learn next

---

5. Green , "(Re-)Turn to Narrative," 28.

week in the next section. This is an admirable goal, for the first step toward narrative preaching is to begin to see how the Bible is connected rather than taking it as a gathering of sayings for us to mine for each week's message or brief series.

If you currently preach your way through an entire book or large section of books, then you have already prepared yourself to become a narrative preacher. If not, I suggest that you continue to preach in the manner to which you have become accustomed—but to start preaching your way through an entire book of the Bible. You need not begin with a large book such as Isaiah or Revelation, but you could easily turn the Epistles or even one of the Gospels into a series. Here are a few suggestions:

- *Preach the whole book.* Don't skip over texts that seem confusing or problematic. Often they present the most challenging and powerful sermonic material because they require you to preach things you might not normally preach or to dig deeper to understand a text that seems either confusing or devoid of good sermon material.

- *Deal with longer sections.* Here you have some wonderful options that create individuality for your series. For instance, if you are preaching your way through the gospel of Luke, chapter 15 would easily divide into three sermons on three parables (lost sheep, lost coin, prodigal son). However, you could also preach on the whole chapter by using the three parables as stories about lostness and God's response to those who are lost. You do not deplete the truth of the chapter by taking a larger section and dealing with it as a whole rather than three parts.

- *Preach the Bible rather than the calendar.* People have said much about churches' use of the calendar. In most congregations, the secular calendar is in focus. We tend to create sermons on love for Valentine's Day, on patriotism for Fourth of July weekend, and so on. Many seminary professors tell their students to use the church calendar and preach according to the themes represented there (Advent, Epiphany, Lent). I propose that you try preaching the Bible instead of the calendar. You will be amazed at how relevant the text will be when you arrive at the text and either look at the calendar, church situation, or current events. To prove this, lay out your preaching calendar in advance of your series. (It makes a great promotional guide for your people.) Let the Holy Spirit lead you in the preparation of the series. You will find that God can work well in advance of the hot-button issues that arrive suddenly, months after you have published and announced your series.[6]

STEPPING-STONE 2
STORY, STORYING, AND STORYTELLING

Studying, teaching, or preaching the whole story of a book will open up new vistas of learning the biblical story. The hand of God is far more evident and powerful in the context of the whole than in ripping out texts so you can preach on what you want rather than on the story of God's handiwork. The key to moving from textualization to story

---

6. I find that only three dates are problematic for preaching through a book and not worrying about the calendar. Those three dates are Christmas (the whole month of Advent), Easter, and Mother's Day. On those dates, your sermon subject has to relate to the holiday in some way.

is narrative preaching. Narrative preaching is built around the idea of the whole, the concept of story, and the ability to tell God's story in your own words. The key ideas of how to do this are *story, storying,* and *storytelling.* We need to understand what these are. Here are the questions we will now seek to understand: What is a story? What is storying? What makes someone a storyteller?

STORY DEFINED

A *story* takes known facts and puts them into a form that we can effectively communicate to others. Story takes a historical narrative and places it in the present tense. Story takes the narrative that God has given us and puts current life and meaning into the events that the Bible relates. Elijah and the confrontation with the prophets of Baal on Mt. Carmel is a historical event. By placing that event in the present and giving it life in the here and now, we transform the event from a narrative to a story. Story brings to life what is past and gives meaning to the present. Livo and Reitz describe the essence of story: "Story is a universal mirror that shows us the 'truth' about ourselves—who and why we are. When we look into this mirror, we see daily routine and mundane circumstance transformed into something profound. 'Story' takes the ordinary and binds it into all of human existence, revealing the significance of the trivial. Through 'story' we can transcend the experience of daily living and know our selves as more enduring than the little occurrences that mark our individual existences."[7]

The story of Elijah is not just about his confrontation with the prophets of Baal. It also is about the crowd's

---

7. Livo and Rietz, *Storytelling,* 4

reaction to his pouring water on a sacrifice that fire is to consume. It is about the feeling of the men pouring water on the sacrifice, men who have endured years of drought and are now pouring out on the ground what must be more precious than gold. Story is filling in the lines between the lines of scripture, without changing the truth and meaning of scripture.

STORYING DEFINED

Storying is more than reading words on a page. We may read a story aloud, but that is not storying. Neither is storying the memorization of a narrative and performing it in front of others, like a soliloquy or monologue on stage. Just as a sermon is not merely a reading of scripture, or the delivery of a memorized speech, storying is not reading a script or becoming an actor. Storying takes what God has revealed and makes it alive, in character, in real time rather than past time. Storying transforms the old story of scripture, either by bringing it from the past into the present (most homileticians call this *application*) or by transporting the audience/congregation into the past to see, feel, touch, smell, and become part of the event. Again, Livo and Reitz illuminate this idea: "Storying is an act. It is what we do to information when we transform it into a story—we story events. Reconfiguration of the memory of an event into the shape of 'story' helps us to better remember the event, even though 'story' may change the memory by *imposing its own shape upon it.*"[8]

In a traditional sermon, the preacher does not harm or distort the scriptural truth but illuminates it in such a way

---

8. Ibid., 5. Italics are mine.

that the Holy Spirit pricks the hearer as the Spirit interprets the truth for each individual life. In storying, the storyteller does not harm or distort the truth but shapes the story so that the truth is illuminated. The thoughts of characters or the addition of implied characters[9] do not change the story any more than the application of principles in a sermon change the scriptural revelation. "Storied events are somehow bigger than themselves, because they have been invested with the greater truth of 'story.'"[10] In storying, we enter into the life of the event rather than looking at the event from the outside. Whether we act as narrator or a character in the story, we become a participant in the event and see the event from inside the story. Like the biblical writers themselves, we become eyewitnesses of a sort. We see the event unfolding and tell others what we are seeing. This is where storytelling and narrative preaching meet. Rather than telling others what someone else has told us, we tell them what we have come to see, hear, and understand ourselves. We become part of the story without changing the events or meaning of the story. This is storying.

STORYTELLING DEFINED

What makes someone a storyteller? The answer to that is much simpler than you think. Storytellers are everywhere. You have met them, worked with them, lived with them, and worshiped with them. They are all around you. Let me give you an example. Have you ever listened to a group of friends talking together? The next time you go out for dinner with a group of friends, see if the following is true. What do they

---

9. In the next chapter, I will share more about implied characters.
10. Ibid.

talk about? It's one story after another. The conversation starts out with people talking about an item on the news. That leads to someone relating a story about how the same thing happened at school that day. Another responds with an event they witnessed at the store a month ago. Finally, the person who first told about the news item shares about what happened to their best friend growing up in rural Indiana. By the time a half hour has passed, people who believe they are not storytellers have told at least a dozen stories on half a dozen subjects! Conclusion? Everyone is a storyteller. All you have to do is get people on the right subject. Most of the time that subject is themselves. We are natural storytellers, given the right subject.

You can weave a story as effectively as the next person. Storytelling lives in you, and the events of your life become the stories of your conversation. You cannot get to know another person without sharing the stories of your life. If you spend any time relating to another person, you will end up talking about the memories, events, priorities, and stories of your life. If some people keep those experiences to themselves and refuse to share their stories with others, we tend to consider them shy, reserved, haughty, or rude. We human beings love to tell stories, especially stories about ourselves.

This natural storytelling ability can be easily transferred to the preaching task. Most of us have already done it. We share illustrations and recall events in our own lives. When first starting out in pulpit ministry, the best stories we can tell are stories about ourselves and our own lives. These stories belong to us because they happened to us, or we observed or experienced them. They require no notes or research. They are in our minds as a picture (or more accurately, as a motion picture), so when we tell them, they unfold naturally. Sometimes we are the main character of our stories, sometimes we are just bit players, and sometimes we are merely the narrators, telling others what we have observed in life. Regardless, the key to our ability to tell such a story is that we are involved with it in some way. Like a group of friends talking, we invite the listeners to join with us in the story. They too become participants in these stories, these illustrations from our lives. Our listeners become part of the crowd that has witnessed the original event, or they begin to see themselves in the role of one of the characters or relate to the story because they have a similar story of their own. We are comfortable with telling a story as long as the story is about us or told from our own perspective. Why? Because we value the story of our own lives and experiences.

WE ARE ALL STORYTELLERS

I would argue that we all think in stories. We certainly dream in stories. As we formulate our own historical memory, we have imaginary motion pictures of the moments and events that make up our past. To tell about ourselves is to share our stories. Stephen Crites says, "The formal quality of experience through time is inherently narrative."[11] In other words, our lives come to our minds and to our mouths in story form rather than as a recitation of facts. To speak of ourselves is to speak in story. To share who we are is to tell others the story of our lives. Jesus inherently knew this and integrated his own story into the sharing of stories with others.

Seminary studies first exposed me to the idea that the story of the Good Samaritan may have been autobiographical rather than a story that Jesus made up. Accept that premise

---

11. Quoted in Eslinger, *Narrative and Imagination*, 5.

31

for a moment; assume that the story is really about Jesus' life. You begin to see the parable as much more powerful than you have ever considered it to be. If Jesus were speaking about his own life and the issues he faced, you begin to see how our lives lay the foundation of how we think about things. Our stories become the basis for the reality of what we think, say, and do.

Yes, we are all storytellers, accomplished and experienced storytellers. We have honed our skills over the years, and we have each developed our own style as storytellers. We have spent half of our lives telling stories about the other half of our lives. We have read books, articles, and magazines only to turn around and tell others about the things we have read. From elementary school onward, we have been encouraged to tell our stories. We have a wealth of experience as narrators of our own lives.

This is why ancient societies practiced the art of storytelling rather than story writing. It is why the New Testament (particularly the Gospels) is structured the way it is. William Barclay describes the catechetical nature of Matthew, arguing that Matthew was organized to be used by teachers as a handbook or guide for newly converted pagan believers.[12] The order is that of story, followed by teaching, followed by story, and so on. Such an order makes story the glue that holds the teaching in place.[13] One can argue that the teaching sections of Matthew are there to help clarify the narrative sections; but to the ancient mind, story was more powerful than propositional truth. An old Hasidic tale relates how an elderly crippled man began to tell the story of

---

12. Barclay, *Introduction to the First Three Gospels*, 168–69.
13. Ibid., 167.

seeing another man healed of his lameness. The storyteller became so enthralled with the story that, unnoticed by his conscious mind, he stood to his feet as the excitement of the story filled his voice. Finally, the man raised his voice in praise to God for healing his friend so many years earlier. As he finished telling the story, he realized that he too had been healed, healed by the power of God working through his friend's story. To the Jews, telling your story was a spiritual experience. To share your story with others was to share your story with God.

This is really the reason God made human beings—because he loves to listen to stories. (Traditional Hasidic saying)[14]

STEPPING-STONE 3
THE STORYTELLING LADDER

Unlike spontaneous combustion, storytelling begins small and grows. Let me be emphatic: *Beginning the journey toward narrative preaching does not require you to begin by preaching a narrative sermon.* First-person preaching is a way to begin, and you can then work your way up the ladder of complexity in your storytelling journey. No one leaps up to the roof. We climb the ladder step by step to get to our desired destination. Since we're using the analogy that storytelling is climbing a ladder, let's begin at the first rung:

- *Series preaching.* As proposed above, this is an excellent way to begin thinking of the Bible in its whole rather than in part. Moving from disconnectedness to wholeness is a powerful way to work your way up

---

14. Livo and Rietz, *Storytelling*, 1.

the storytelling ladder. It will at least get you off the ground and onto the ladder!

- *Illustrations.* As a preacher, you already have experience telling stories in your sermons. You call them illustrations. Begin by looking for illustrations that are stories. These are great starters as well as gripping conclusions to effective sermons. Whether they come from your own life, from books or newspapers, or even through a subscription illustration service, learn how to tell those stories in your own words and with your own style. How can you know when you are telling stories well? If you tell an illustration and no one moves, if you go through a story and no one coughs or gets up to leave, if you can hear that proverbial pin drop and feel the eyes of the congregation fixed on you, then you have entered into that wonderful arena of storytelling. You begin to sense the power of story.

- *Restatement.* It is a mistake to assume that by having the scripture passage read before we preach, we have sufficiently exposed the congregation to the text so that they understand or remember it. After a sermon text is read, you should retell it before you get into the heart of the sermon. Haddon Robinson calls this technique "restatement" and says that it produces two important results: clarity and impressing truth on the listeners. "Listeners, unlike readers, must get what is said when we say it. They cannot go back and hear it again."[15] By retelling the biblical story in your own words or by giving additional background

---

15. Robinson, *Biblical Preaching*, 138.

information in a narrative way, we recap the story and impress it upon our hearers. This not only allows us to build up our narrative storytelling ability; it also fixes the story in the mind of the listener. Robinson explains: "Restatement differs from repetition. Repetition says the same thing in the same words; restatement says the same thing in different words."[16] If you have a narrative text that someone has already read aloud, restate the story in your own words. This enables the listener to hear the story read and to hear the story told. Such restatements will impress the story of the text on the reader's heart and mind.

- *Imagineering.*[17] It is not a huge leap from restating a story to imagineering it. Imagineering means using creativity in retelling the story of a biblical text. Scripture lends itself to imagineering in a variety of ways. When we use our imaginations to tell a story rather than reading it, we are imagineering, using creativity to narrate the story in our own way. For years, preachers and teachers have been concerned about the warning of Revelation 22:18[18] and have not wanted to tell anything in their narrative that isn't a direct quote from the Scriptures themselves. I fully understand and appreciate this concern. Heretical groups have changed and rearranged Scripture in order to dilute its truth and tamper with

---

16. Ibid., 139.

17. Walt Disney coined this term when he sought to wed together the engineering and creative functions of the Disney concept. It is now a well-accepted term for creativity in thinking, used not only by the Disney Corporation but also by a host of other enterprises and Web sites.

18. "I warn everyone who hears the words of the prophecy of this book: If anyone adds anything to them, God will add to him the plagues described in this book."

its message, thus doing much damage to the gospel. This is not what I am encouraging you to do. Make sure you understand the biblical text before you try any kind of imagineering with it. After all, sermonic storytelling is not intended to take the place of scripture but to make the true story come alive and compel the listener to engage with the story in their own minds and lives, compelling them to read it and apply it to themselves. Jesus often remarked, "You have heard it said..." On such occasions, his purpose was not merely to quote the text but to explain its meaning. In the same way, we can communicate a scripture passage in narrative form without directly quoting the text as long as it does not harm the text or deviate from the meaning and message of the text. We can do this in various ways.

For instance, if you are preaching on the Ten Commandments, read the commandment you are using as your text and then tell the story of the passage. You might relate the setting of Moses on the mountain or give a brief background of the wilderness wanderings that brought the nation to this point. You might even describe the scene as the nation in debauchery down below, and the hand of God handing down the moral foundation for that same nation.

The story of feeding the five thousand might enable you to tell, in your own words, what took place in that event. Don't worry about memorizing the story so you can tell it verbatim; you've already done that by reading the text. Concentrate instead on describing the event as it replays in your mind. Here are some lines that can help to introduce a retelling of the passage in your own words:

Imagine, if you will...

- *Example*: Imagine, if you will, Andrew finding a willing boy with the lunch his mother packed him.

Picture with me the scene...

- *Example:* Picture with me the scene of a hungry crowd that came to hear Jesus but could only hear the rumblings of their own stomachs.

In your mind's eye...

- *Example:* In your mind's eye visualize the moment when Jesus looked at Philip and said, "How shall we feed them?"

Put yourself in the story...

- *Example:* Put yourself in the story. Can you see what the crowd looked like, how young the boy is, and how perplexed the disciples are?

STEPPING-STONE 4
TELLING STORIES IN THE SHOWER

Maybe the biggest change you make in moving from propositional teaching to narrative preaching is in how you prepare the sermon. In the traditional approach to sermon preparation, everything begins by reading the text. James Earl Massey, former dean of the chapel at Tuskegee, was one of my mentors in preaching. His admonition for beginning sermon preparation stays with me today. His unalterable rule for sermon preparation was that it must begin with reading the scripture text. The preacher then moves on to reading the text. Finally, after reading and rereading the text, the preacher should read the text. Dr. Massey believed that a preacher preparing a sermon should read the biblical text often enough that, even when looking up from the page, the preacher can still visualize the text. The same steps are necessary for becoming a narrative preacher. Narrative preaching begins with the biblical text and requires a thorough immersion in the text. So the first step in narrative preparation does not differ from the first step in traditional sermon preparation.

The second step takes a different tack. In traditional sermon preparation, the next step is writing. Whether you start with compiling word studies or commentary work or recording your own reaction to the text, you are writing down your thoughts. Putting things down on paper allows you to review and redirect your thoughts. It is a tried-and-true process. However, in narrative preaching, you must aim to tell the story. So rather than making notes, your next step is to try telling the story. The same rules apply. When you write down your thoughts about the biblical text, the most fruitful approach is to write down whatever comes to your mind—whether it makes sense, contradicts the point you just wrote down, or borders on heresy. You just write down whatever comes to mind. You will sort out your thoughts later. This step helps you think creatively about the passage. What thoughts come to your mind as you contemplate the meaning of the text? Too many students of the Word skip this step and go directly to the Bible commentators, who have thought deeply about the text and written down their thoughts about the passage. However, the Holy Spirit can certainly use you (after all, the Spirit called you to preach and/or teach). You can think creatively and insightfully about the Word of God.

In developing a sermon of propositional truth, you must put down on paper what comes to mind from your research, word study, or contemplation. In narrative preaching, the story is the thing. So, rather than writing down your thoughts, you speak them. You begin by telling the story. Tell it out loud. Thinking a story doesn't work. If you have ever read a text silently that you must eventually read aloud, you know that there is a considerable difference between thinking a text inwardly and reading that text aloud. The same thing is true about narrative preaching. Writing down a sermon story that you are going to tell aloud does not work. Just tell the story. As you do, you will come upon thoughts and ideas that take you places you would never go if left to your own writing. Speaking involves a different mental dynamic than writing. Let your thoughts go wherever they may take you. If you run into a brick wall because you lack information about the story, make a list of things you need to research, but don't let that take the place of talking through the story. If you suspect that your telling is not completely accurate, write down a note to check your facts—but continue to tell the story. Let the narrative flow.

To a narrative preacher, the shower can become a spiritual place. Anyplace where you can be alone and tell the story aloud, letting the narrative freely flow from your heart and mind, develops the skill of storytelling. You may spend a few more dollars on hot water, but you may also find that you possess an imagination that can heat up your sermons for those who listen to the Word of God.

STEPPING-STONE 5
DEAD ENDS LEAD TO NEW HIGHWAYS

Just because narrative preaching emphasizes telling stories, you are not excused from doing thoughtful research. Research is as crucial to storytelling as it is for any kind of sermon preparation. One Sunday, after I had told the story of Gideon in a first-person narrative sermon, a parishioner came up to me and said she was thrilled with the sermon. She had followed along in the scripture text, and I had made only two errors! (Believe me, people check up on preachers!) On another occasion, I told the story of Jesus' birth and placed it in a cave that belonged to shepherds who used it for birthing sheep. People were fascinated by this unusual concept. It came from research I had done concerning the most likely places Jesus may have been born.

Research for narrative preaching occurs at a different place in the preparatory cycle than it does in traditional sermon work. Traditionally, you start with the scripture text and try to understand the main point so that you can write down an exposition of the theme. In narrative sermon preparation, you begin with the story. What are the real details of the story? Concentrate on your ability to tell the whole story, accurately and colorfully. Which characters are involved and when do they speak? Instead of studying the implications of the textual message as you read the text, concentrate on the story itself.

The next step is to tell the story out loud. This step will spawn much of the research you do. When you tell the story out of your heart, mind, and imagination, you will undoubtedly say things that surprise you. After saying them, it is normal for a storyteller to ask, "Is that really true?" Don't worry about the accuracy of your statement at that point. Simply write it down and use it as your list for later research. Some things you say as you verbally elaborate the story may not be accurate, but they may spur you to learn additional information that will enhance the story. Accuracy is crucial, but accuracy can only be achieved if you are willing to look at all aspects of the text. In traditional sermon preparation, you may write down things that you ultimately find do not jibe with the text or sound theology; nevertheless, writing them down causes you to seek out the answer. The same is true in narrative sermon preparation, but it arises out of telling the story rather than from writing down ideas about the text.

Another aspect of narrative sermon preparation is dealing with dead ends in your story. You go along telling your story, and some thought takes you to a dead end. It seems to be a dead end because you have no additional information that can help you assess the situation and continue with the story. I was developing the story of Elijah and the widow of Zarephath when I realized that I knew nothing about where Zarephath was or what kind of city it was (1 Kings 17). I began to research the issue and found, to my surprise, that the town was not in Israel. So God sent Elijah out of his own nation to help a Gentile widow when all of Israel was in a drought; that fact was quite instructive for the development of the story. Out of my research, other pieces of information arose that added to the development of the story. Dead ends can lead you to open highways of information and story development. They are gateways to knowledge and highways to new thoughts.

CONCLUSION

As with any methodology, you may find that some of these stepping-stones are more helpful than others. It is certainly not an exhaustive list of steps for preparing narrative sermons, but these steps will help lead you through your first experience of narrative preaching. It will also enable you to begin slowly and then move from retooling your existing sermon style and preparation to doing a truly narrative sermon. Remember the stepping-stones:

1. Preach wholes instead of holes.

2. Realize that you are a storyteller.

3. Begin your storytelling adventure by using the storytelling ladder.

4. Speak your stories out loud—in the shower if you dare!

5. Base your narratives on sound research and move from dead ends to new highways.

Once you have followed these stepping-stones, you are ready to begin preaching in narrative. Next, you need to learn how to develop a story by developing a character. That is the next step in becoming a narrative preacher.

3

CHARACTERS IN THE SERMON
MOVING FROM SNAPSHOTS
TO MOTION PICTURES

I love to tell the story—because I know 'tis true,
It satisfies my longings as nothing else can do.

At any preaching service today, you are likely to find in the bulletin, in the pew, or on an overhead screen an outline (with blank lines to fill) of the sermon for the morning. I even attended one church where the sermon notes had been three-hole punched so that the listener might slip them into a notebook for future reference. A few years ago, our church was going through the Forty Days of Purpose, a program based on Rick Warren's book *The Purpose-Driven Life*. The materials provided to the church included a fill-in outline of the suggested sermon for the week for us to print in our bulletin. I started using these, adapting them to the sermons I actually preached for the forty days. After the program was over, one of the educators in the church strongly encouraged me to continue the practice with whatever sermons I preached in the future, so I continued the practice. After using it for some months, I began to question its value. My question still is, how valuable a learning tool is the printed sermon outline?

Let me suggest an unscientific but simple exercise for you to do with members of your congregation. It consists of two questions. On Wednesday night (or Sunday morning), ask those who heard your sermon the previous Sunday to write down any of the main points made during the message. Second, have them write down any illustration that you used in that sermon. I can almost guarantee that if they remember anything about your most recent sermon, it will not be any of the three points you outlined, put up on the screen in PowerPoint, or agonized over during your sermon preparation. If they remember anything, it will be one of your illustrations.

One year during Advent, I decided to do a sermon series using the method of first-person narrative. My son Jonathan, home from graduate school for the holidays, heard one of those sermons. Six months later, while talking about the series with some friends from another state, I tried to remember the subject matter for each of the sermons in the series. I recalled the first four but could not remember the final sermon in the series. Immediately, Jonathan not only supplied me with the main character from whose perspective I had told the story but also reminded me of the main thrust the story line had taken. Why is it that the modern mind learns so well from illustrations but struggles so much with lists of ideas and concepts? Simply put, stories and pictures have a far more profound effect on the mind than lists or statements of ideas. If you want to be contemporary in your preaching, then know this: research has repeatedly confirmed that everyone from the buster generation to postmoderns learns better through narrative, whether told with sophisticated media technology or by a single storyteller, than they do through any other kind of medium.[1]

---

1. Barna, *Baby Busters*, 71.

Advertising executives have embraced this idea. Watch any commercial on television or attend any cinematic production, and it will be filled with images that do not stay on the screen for more than a few seconds.[2] Communicators who connect effectively with postmodern culture use multiple images rather than one image, and they leave those images on the screen for one second or less. I recently attended a movie theater where, after arriving early, I was able to watch the advertising that goes on the screen before the movie. (We were the first ones in the theater and had the joy of watching the advertising several times!) This gave me an opportunity to observe how the audience reacted. First, several of the advertisers had supplied a video clip rather than a slide show. The audience's interest level increased dramatically when the advertising messages went from slides to moving pictures. Second, viewers needed five to ten seconds to read all of the information contained on a slide. In the video presentations, the images changed every second or less. The slides were designed to share information and detail. The video clips were designed to tell a story and place an idea in viewers' minds. For me, the experience was a revelation. I kept wondering which format was more like the typical sermon. Are preachers in the pulpit to share information and detail, or are we there to tell a story and place within the minds, hearts, and souls of others an idea about who God is and what he has for us?

---

2. Turn on your television set and watch some commercials for a bit. Time the images on the screen and you will see that they rarely stay static for more than three seconds. If the advertisement is aimed at postmoderns, it will be even less. Turn on MTV, watch the movement of images during a music video and you will be amazed at how fast the screen moves and the images change. It is even more frequent than the commercials designed for baby boomers.

There is a wide chasm between the principles of traditional rhetoric and modern advertising. When Cicero wrote about rhetoric more than two thousand years ago in his treatise *On the Orator*, he listed five basic principles of oratory that have become the foundation for sermon construction ever since. His fivefold plan broke a speech down into the following concepts:

1. *Invention.* First is the process of discovering what needs to be said. For the homiletician, this is the hermeneutical and exegetical process.

2. *Arrangement.* At this stage, the speaker takes information and puts it into a persuasive form. The speaker tries to achieve flow, transition, and order.

3. *Style.* The speaker considers the artful application of language and seeks unique ways to express the ideas to be communicated.

4. *Memory.* This involves the speaker remembering what needs to say in the order (arrangement) that has been predetermined. Preachers who master this concept are able to preach without notes.

5. *Delivery.* The homiletical task involves delivering the message in a style that will engage the listener.[3]

Contrast these concepts of rhetoric with the basic modern-day principles of advertising. You will see that a tremendous shift has taken place. All the advertising textbooks tell us an ad has several jobs to do:

---

3. Cicero, *On the Orator*, 31; Loscalzo, "Rhetoric," 410.

1. to attract attention to itself;

2. to enlist the reader's interest;

3. to create desire, or to capitalize on existing desire, for the product or service being advertised;

4. to persuade the reader to buy the product or service or to accept the idea being advanced;

5. to show him how and where he can buy the product or service or to direct him to some specific course of action.[4]

In comparing the two sets of communication principles, several differences are evident: (1) Modern advertisers assume that the advertising message begins with the consumer. Attracting attention, enlisting interest, and creating desire are at the forefront of the advertisers' preparation. On the other hand, rhetoric begins with the information. The rhetorician tries to discover, arrange, and express this information to an audience. (2) Advertisers see the world in pictures; rhetoricians see things in words and persuasive concepts. (3) Advertisers want their listeners to remember a product so they will buy and use it. Rhetoricians want listeners to remember concepts so they can present them persuasively to others.

What does all this mean? Without question, the effective use of language is a crucial issue for the preacher. Equally important, if not of surpassing importance, is sound biblical exegesis, which ensures that we are preaching truth and not heresy. However, if we do not understand the basic differences between how rhetoricians persuade and how the

---

4. Nelson, *Design of Advertising*, 11.

advertising media persuade people, we miss the opportunity to engage this generation in meaningful dialogue with the biblical text. We must move from idea snapshots, represented by fill-in-the-blank outlines, to the motion-picture concept of story. People are not learning from the sermons most of us are preaching. The postmodern generation is staying away from church services in astounding numbers. We must open ourselves to the possibility that people learn today in ways that are different from the way they learned in the 1950s.

THE CASE FOR LEARNING THROUGH STORY

After Jerry Lucas finished his outstanding career and retired as one of the greatest basketball players of all time (both collegiate and professional), he began to teach and write about how people learn. His revolutionary method (he calls it the Lucas Learning System) continues to astound anyone who sits under his teaching. The system is based on the principle that we learn by pictorial association. Over the years he has created systems to help people remember facts with mnemonics, and he has employed series of pictures that allow people to visualize what they want to memorize.[5] Recently, my wife and I set out to memorize the book of Mark using the Lucas Learning System. We were astounded at what the mind can do with pictures. By putting together a series of pictures that represent other things, it becomes possible to remember long lists of items (even biblical verses) by picturing them in your mind.

During the audiotape instructions for the memorization of Mark, Lucas tells of the discovery he made years ago

5. Lucas, *Learning How to Learn.*

concerning how the great Greek orators would remember speeches that lasted four to six hours.[6] Using picture memorization, the Greeks would key that to their house furniture to keep their thoughts flowing. They would picture a room in their house and place an idea on top of the item nearest the entrance. Moving around the room, they would place another idea on the next piece of furniture, and the next, and so on. This trick kept their memories on track and their speeches moving forward.[7] By picturing ideas, they could dramatize their points and keep them in order. Why would they go to such lengths? Why not just write the ideas down and take the notes with them? Simply put, writing was expensive and difficult. So the leaders of ancient societies (even biblical ones) avoided writing things down. They were oral cultures.

Even to a greater degree than the ancient Greeks, the Jews believed in the power of the spoken story. Written messages cannot give you the inflection and tone of the writer. You can read the thoughts of an author, but you cannot see the author's face. In contrast, a speaker can convey not only thoughts and ideas but also passion, conviction, and emphasis. We best communicate these by speaking, not writing. And we best accomplish them without the traditional didactic form.

Gene Roddenberry created a whole media phenomenon by developing the *Star Trek* television series (1966–69). Roddenberry's basic idea for the series was to take modern-day issues and put them in a futuristic setting in order to start a dialogue about those issues, which he could not address explicitly on television. Subsequent *Star Trek* writers picked up on this idea and communicated controversial

---

6. Lucas, *His Word*, 54ff.

7. This is one of the key ways in which rhetoricians would fulfill Cicero's fourth point about memorization.

ideas through their stories. In an amazing episode of the later television series *Star Trek: The Next Generation*, Paul Winfield played a character called Captain Dathon in an episode titled "Darmok." In this story, Dathon and Captain Picard find themselves together on a planet where they must learn to trust one another even though they cannot communicate with one another. The problem is not that they speak two entirely different languages like English and Russian, but that they have entirely different forms of language. What Dathon says is understandable, but the meaning of his words and phrases are not.

As the episode reaches its climax, Picard begins to realize that Dathon is communicating not in concepts but in stories. His repetitive phrases are shorthand for some event or myth that, in his culture, is so well-known that a mere reference to the story conveys what the speaker means.[8] In his culture, Dathon recalls great events and stories in order to share his emotions, feelings, and information. The title of the episode "Darmok" refers to a great battle fought by Dathon's ancestors. It was an emblem of courage and brotherhood. As the story ends, Picard is finally able to communicate with Dathon as Dathon dies from his wounds suffered in combat. When Picard returns to the *Enterprise*, he hails the flagship of his fallen comrade and, by using story references, he communicates with Dathon's second in command the tragic yet heroic death of his commander, Captain Dathon. Imagine living in an entire culture that bases all of its

---

8. We do this all the time in church circles. We use a type of shorthand and assume others will know exactly what we mean. The truth is that when we are addressing a congregation of people, many of whom don't know the shorthand, and use our inbred phrases, we end up sounding as foreign as Captain Dathon sounded to Picard.

communication on stories. You may not have to imagine. We are nearly there in our society today. We learn much better through stories than we do through the written word alone. If that were not true, we would not spend as much time with television sets and movies as we do today.

Years ago, I was trained in Evangelism Explosion, the groundbreaking evangelism program put together by Dr. James Kennedy. In teaching us how to communicate the gospel, Kennedy shared a principle that I have seen quoted and used in many different disciplines. He said that one's words communicate only 7 percent of a message, tone of voice conveys 38 percent, and body language carries 55 percent. This means that body language and tone of voice convey 93 percent of a message that someone communicates. To preachers, this is a devastating insight; we spend so much of our time and energy trying to craft the right words to communicate our messages that we are somewhat unnerved by the idea that communication is largely a matter of voice inflection and physical gestures. We need something more than words to adequately inform and persuade this generation about the grand truths of the Word of God. We need to move from snapshots of facts to motion pictures of life.

THE MOVEMENT TOWARD NARRATIVE

To move toward narrative preaching, we must stop *looking* at the biblical text. I do not mean by this to denigrate the importance of observation. It's just that we have been trained to look at a scripture text and try to see what's in it. This is a one-dimensional task. Even when we have been encouraged to mine the text or to go deeper into the story, we have remained outside the story. It has continued to be a one-dimensional process. To engage in narrative preaching, we must retrain our minds to see the scriptural story not as a one-dimensional snapshot of a historical event but as part of our own living story. When we become part of the biblical story and it becomes part of us, we move from snapshot to motion picture, from one-dimensional thinking to multi-dimensional involvement. Let me describe two examples of how this works, one a biblical example and the other media related.

The book of Acts is a two-act play that changes main characters in midstream. For the first twelve chapters the actions, ideas, and understandings of Peter command the stage. From chapter 13 onward, the apostle Paul and his missionary journeys become the focus. We cannot deny the dramatic narrative of the book of Acts. It is as if this divinely inspired author understood that the prime consideration for engaging his readers was to concentrate on story. Having already written the story of Jesus Christ in his gospel, Luke continues to tell his story from the perspective of the characters that dominated the apostolic church. At some points in the narrative, Luke himself enters the story and tells it from his own eyewitness account.[9] At other points, Luke narrates the unfolding story of the Holy Spirit as related to him by Paul and other eyewitnesses. (Luke clearly states in the preamble to his gospel that he has sought out eyewitnesses to the stories he tells.) In both cases, Luke relates these events from inside the story rather than outside the story. He either enters the story himself as a member of Paul's entourage or enters the story of the eyewitnesses' accounts by becoming their narrator. Like the writers of other biblical material, Luke sees

---

9. These famous "we" passages begin in Acts 16 and crop up several times as Luke becomes the traveling companion of Paul on some of his journeys (see note 12).

himself in the narrative even when he is not physically present at the event.[10]

Traditional sermon preparation encourages us to remain outside the biblical text and bring our keen analytical abilities to the narrative. Narrative preaching invites us to enter the biblical text and see the story from the inside out.

The second example comes from television. Stephen King's book *The Dead Zone* has become an original show produced for the USA Network. The main character, John Smith, suffers an accident that leaves him in a coma for years. When he finally emerges from the coma, he finds that his mind no longer works like yours and mine. He now has visions triggered when he comes in contact with someone or something. Whether you accept the premise of the program or not, the way in which it portrays John Smith's visions is instructive for our purpose. Whenever Smith touches someone or something, he experiences a vision in which he becomes a participant in the story of that person or thing. He enters into their story. He may see an event that is about to occur or something that has taken place in the past. Smith enters the story in one of two ways. He either becomes a neutral observer, walking around in the event he sees, or he becomes one of the main characters in the story. After he sees the vision, he returns to the real world of today and begins to interact with people who were the subject of his vision.

---

10. The Old Testament books of history are replete with examples of the writers entering into the story. From the final climactic scene of Moses' death told not by Moses but by a writer, and on to the writers of both Kings and Chronicles as they experience the actions of prophets, kings, and battles—the historical sections of the Old Testament show the author entering the story. In the New Testament the gospel writers are all, with the exception of Luke, participants to some, most, or all of the events they describe. However, they write not a first-person account but a story into which each of them has entered.

Far-fetched though it is, the program is instructive about how we as preachers must enter the story of Scripture in order to truly communicate it. Once we enter the story, we will no longer see the event as a mere snapshot of an historical moment but begin to experience the story from the inside out. It moves from snapshot to motion picture. Even when we step back out of the story and interact with our congregation in the real world of today, what we have seen and experienced within the story will influence us.

Understanding this concept is crucial if you are to begin preaching from a narrative point of view. Narrative preaching demands that, like Luke, you become part of the entourage of the story. You must begin asking questions of the text from inside it rather than outside it. In narrative preaching, you learn to describe how it feels to be the victim of a drought; this becomes crucial to understanding the story of Elijah. You experience what it is like to travel a dusty road without water and finally come upon the widow of Zarephath, whom you ask for a drink. This is not ancillary information but goes to the heart of the story. Why? Because when you enter a story, how the people in the story see, think, feel, and react become integral to your understanding of the story. Once you have moved into the story, how you relate to what you find there becomes the next step in your work as a narrative preacher.

STEP 1: MOVING INTO THE TEXT
The Narrator Approach

One way to move into the biblical text is to become part of the story but not one of the characters in the story. You become the narrator. The narrator tells the story without being part of it. Most preachers do this in some sense when describing the biblical story in a typical sermon. If you are preaching on the story of the prodigal son and retell the story in your own words, you have become the narrator. Whether you tell the story in a quick two-minute summary or take twenty minutes to flesh out the story, you are describing in real terms the motion picture that is the parable of the lost son. You enter the story from above and become an inspired reporter, telling others what you see in the moving picture of the biblical text. You picture what the prodigal looks like. You imagine the house, the pigsty, the killing of the fatted calf, the color and size of the ring placed on the prodigal's finger when he is welcomed home. You do not give a word-for-word recitation of the passage (often someone has done this before preaching by simply reading the text to the congregation). Instead, you become the storyteller. You begin to tell the story as you picture it in your mind's eye. And like a group of artists in front of a bowl of fruit, each preacher's rendering of a text will come out differently than the others'.[11] The topic is the same, the text is the same, but each teller has a different perspective on the story.

---

11. In a real sense, this is similar to what men like Kenneth Taylor and John Peterson have done in producing the paraphrases of *The Living Bible* (Taylor, 1971) and *The Message* (Peterson, 1993). These hugely popular paraphrases have caught the attention of both preacher and parishioner because they have a different perspective on the narrative of Scripture. I share this because the storyteller still has a definite responsibility to be true to the text while at the same time taking opportunity to add to the story details that his sanctified imagination allows him to see in the story. One must never use narrative preaching as a license to do harm to the Scripture any more than one would allow a three-point sermon to take from the text truths that are not part of the text. In addition, narrative preaching has the same theological ethics that any other textual sermon has.

When you narrate a biblical story, it not only comes to the congregation in a form different from the text; it also comes in a form different from how they have imagined the scene in their minds. As the narrator, you get to choose how you will describe the characters in the story. Is the prodigal immature or prideful? Is he rebelling against the strict Judaism of his father, or is he Jewish in name only and never truly practiced the faith? Have friends in other ways tempted him so that now he wants to strike out on his own to see what he can find? Is he a young man with pure motives and high ideals who succumbs to the wiles of sudden wealth and popularity? If you are the narrator, you get to share your vision of the spiraling descent of the prodigal from a rich landowner's son to small farmer's pig feeder. The text does not reveal the full details of this degradation, but in your mind's eye the story begins to unfold.

Some texts require little imagination but simply an accurate retelling of the story. A Father's Day sermon about King David as a father will powerfully portray the negative effects of poor parenting skills. Telling the story of Ruth to those who have been divorced, widowed, or abandoned by someone they loved can provide encouraging hope and renew your listeners' trust in the patient faithfulness in God. In a society enamored with sexual temptations, telling how Esther became queen and was faithful to God, thus saving the Jews from genocide, can be powerful to teenagers struggling with the belief that having sex outside marriage will make someone a real man or a real woman. Becoming the narrator of these stories only requires that you adhere faithfully to the story that God has already written about these lives. Like the writers of Scripture, you too become the conduit for bringing to us the age-old story of God's work among us. All you have to do is tell the story. All you have to do is enter the story.

Have you ever noticed how differently people react to illustrations told from a first-person perspective rather than a third-person perspective? People are always interested in what happens to other people, but when they know that the illustration was lived by the speaker, it takes on an even greater import. In a first-person illustration, the impact of the story dramatically increases. None of us has the opportunity to share the biblical narrative as people who actually lived those events. But in narrative preaching, you get as close as possible to telling the story *as though* you really were there. In narrative preaching, you can tell the story *as if* you were a participant in the event. That, however, will require us to move even deeper into the narrative. Now we must begin to learn how to develop character.

STEP 2: MOVING INTO THE STORY
BECOMING THE MAIN CHARACTER

Where you stand when you enter the story makes a difference in how you tell the story. If you stand above the story and relate what you see, you don't interact with the events of the story. You become a reporter, recording the events as they take place. This is the role of the narrator. But what if you became a participant in the event? Narrative preaching allows you to become an active part of the story. This personal interaction with the events lets you explore a whole new realm of insights that preachers do not usually see as germane to the preaching task. This is a movement not just into the text but also a movement into the story of the text. Rather than your merely reporting the events, those events actually affect you.

You move from a third-person reportorial stance to a first-person interactive stance. In other words, you go from being Luke the historian, writing down the stories of others, to Luke the traveling companion of Paul, writing down the events that he heard, saw, and in which he became a partner.[12]

Telling a sermon from within the text is a fascinating experience. You choose a character from the text and begin to interact with the story as it unfolds. But which character should you choose?

Perhaps the most prevalent form of this technique portrays the main character in narrative sections of Scripture. Main characters are the easiest to develop because the text has already fleshed them out. The main character is almost always involved in a significant part of the story. Therefore, the preacher has a wealth of material and will have to decide what to leave out rather than imagining more details to stuff into the story (which could be dangerous from an ethical stance anyway). All you have to do is fill in a few missing pieces. If good exegesis begins by asking questions of the text, then good character development begins by asking questions of the character: How does that feel? Why would you do that? What are you thinking at this point? Why don't you realize what the consequences of your actions will be?

By going into the text to develop the character, you become presentational rather than just representational. Famed actress and acting teacher Uta Hagen has explained it this way:

---

12. Acts 16:9–18; 20:5–21:18; 27:1–28:16; as cited in many commentaries.

The Representational actor deliberately chooses to imitate or illustrate the character's behavior. The Presentational actor attempts to reveal human behavior through the use of himself, through an understanding of himself and consequences, and an understanding of the character he is portraying. The Representational actor finds a form based on an objective result for the character, which he then carefully watches as he executes it. The Presentational actor trusts that a form will result from identification with the character and the discovery of his character's actions, and works on stage for a moment-to-moment subjective experience.[13]

Hagan advocates the presentational style of acting. I think this approach works best in the pulpit as well. You are not trying to imitate a biblical character but portray one. In choosing a main character as your focus, you typically have a wealth of material from which to draw an understanding of the character. I cannot mimic an Elijah, Jonah, or Peter, but I can present them as I understand them from the Scriptures.

If you choose to tell the story as a main character, you should ask yourself several key questions as that character. For example, let's consider some of the basic questions you might ask if you are telling the parable of the prodigal son.

QUESTIONS THAT AID IN DEVELOPING A CHARACTER
Background questions
If you have ever taken an acting class, your professor probably called this the back story. These questions attempt

---

13. Hagan, *Respect for Acting*, 11–12.

to understand how the story got to the point where the biblical narrative begins. Your answers to these questions may never become the bulk of what you preach, but they will certainly help you in understanding the main character you have chosen. Hagen created six primary questions for an actor looking at developing a character in her book *Respect for Acting*:

1. Who am I? (What is my present state of being? How do I perceive myself? What am I wearing?)

2. What are the circumstances? (What time is it—the year, time, period, season, or day? At what time does my selected life begin?) Where am I? (In what city, neighborhood, building, and room do I find myself? Or in what landscape if outdoors?) What surrounds me? (What is the immediate landscape? The weather? The condition of the place and the nature of the objects in it?)

3. What are my relationships? (How do I stand in relationship to the circumstances, the place, the objects, and the *other people* related to my circumstances?)

4. What do I want? (What is my main objective? What do I want from others in the scene? What is my immediate need or objective?)

5. What are my obstacles? (What stands in the way of what I want? How will I overcome it?)

6. What do I do when I get what I want? (What do I do to get my objective? What is my behavior? What are my actions? [Keep them small and specific.] How far am I willing to go to reach my objective?)[14]

---

14. This summary is taken from Meyer, "Six Steps."

I realize that these are acting tools and not sermonic tools. They do, however, provide a foundation for many things you can do to aid your development of character. They may not all apply in the case of the story you are seeking to tell or the character you want to flesh out, but they are valuable tools for looking inside the character. For instance, in the story of the prodigal son,[15] there are some key questions you should ask of the main character:

- What has been the relationship between my father and me?

- What happened between my father and me that brought this confrontation to a head?

- What has been the relationship between my older brother and me?

- How old am I? How old is my older brother?

- How rich is my father, and by extension, how wealthy will I become upon receiving my portion of the inheritance?

Conflict questions

Drama is about conflict. The first task in interpreting a narrative passage is to try to determine what conflict gives rise to confrontation in the text. If you have ever heard an actor in a play or movie ask the director, "What's my motivation?" you have heard a simple form of this question. In your own mind, you need to determine why a character is doing what he or she is doing. Again, from the prodigal son parable:

---

15. By using a parable, I run the risk of being criticized because this is not necessarily a true story but only a parable story. I assure you that the process I share here is applicable to both parable stories and historical stories. The use of parable is convenient for instruction not integral to the process.

- Why do I want to leave the ranch?

- Am I leaving because of problems or because I want adventure?

- Am I motivated to strike out on my own by boredom, frustration, excitement, or the desire to find myself?

- Am I negatively reacting to the strict nature of my father's religious beliefs?

Questions to flesh out the story

One of the unique questions that you can effectively answer in narrative preaching, which can be quite dangerous in traditional preaching, is how to flesh out a story. In traditional preaching, this can easily lead to eisegesis (reading one's own ideas into the text). However, in narrative preaching, the storytelling role gives the preacher greater latitude in filling in details not readily seen in the text. The storytelling nature of the narrative sermon gives license to this kind of question-and-answer process.

- How does the prodigal descend into the pits of sin? Few people fall off a cliff into the pits of sin. Most descend down a long, spiraling staircase of poor choices and deeply held insecurities to arrive at the bottom. How did the prodigal get there?

- How aware was he of his own fall?

- Did any of his friends or family try to save him from the fall?

- Did his father or brother ever go and try to get him to come back to the ranch?

Turning-point questions

Narratives have points where the story takes a dramatic turn. These turning points relieve or create tension in the story. How a character navigates between these turning points gives crucial insight. Jesus' parables are full of tremendous turning points. Asking how you (or the main character) would react to the situation will give you even greater insight into the story.

- What does the prodigal do with his inheritance? The passage gives some idea but no details. (This question takes you from the turning point of asking for the inheritance and navigates you toward the next turning point, which is his loss of the inheritance.)

- How much does the prodigal understand about his social, economic, and spiritual slide as it is going on? How does he react along the way to the loss of his money, friends, self-worth, and meaning? How does he get the job on the farm, slopping hogs? (These questions take you from the turning point of his high living to the job in the pigpen.)

- What is the prodigal feeling as he is walking home? Is he practicing his humility speech? What does he expect the reaction of his father to be? (This question takes you from the turning point of realizing his plight to the redeeming moment in front of his father.)

Each of these is a turning point; there may well be more than the ones I've listed. How you navigate your character from one turning point to the next turning point determines how the character develops in your mind and, eventually, in the sermon.

Key-moment questions

In every dramatic story, there is a key moment upon which the story hinges. For instance, in the story of the prodigal son, we find this moment when he decides to return to his father's house and become a servant. These are some of the great teaching points in any parable or narrative of Scripture. Asking questions of this key moment not only provides you with insight into how the character in the story reacted but also helps you understand how others (and many of them will be in the congregation) might react to such a moment.

- Describe the moment when you came to yourself.

- How does it feel to realize that you no longer control your life and to grasp that if you are ever to save yourself from this predicament, it will have to come through humility and sacrifice?

- Is it crushing to come face-to-face with the inevitable results of the sinful choices you have made? Or is it a freeing experience to be able to move beyond the wrong choices to a new, hopeful future?

Resolution questions

One of the marvelous features of biblical stories is that they inevitably resolve themselves, often leaving us a powerful message. This is true especially for parables, but it is equally true for the whole of Scripture. These questions aim to uncover the main character's reactions to the event. How a main character reacts to the resolution of the story is a key component in understanding what the implications are for that character now that the conflict has been resolved.

- How did you react to the lavish welcome your father and his servants gave you?

- What was your long-term reaction to your reinstatement in the family? (Remember that the father makes it clear to the elder brother that the prodigal's return does not put the latter back in line for more inheritance. What he has squandered is gone and will not be replaced.)

- Do you and elder brother ever resolve your differing personalities and priorities? If so, how long does it take? If not, why not?

Using these simple questions can lead to a tremendous amount of material that you can use for preaching. My son Joel, in graduate school studying to be an actor, tells me that the joy of acting is in the choices you make with the character you are portraying. We can experience that same kind of joy in preaching. Taking a text and preaching from it is a Spirit-guided, individually gifted act. That's why two preachers can preach from the same text and come up with entirely different sermons (as actors will come up with entirely different persons, though they are portraying the same character in a play).

Years ago, I gave an undergraduate college class in homiletics the assignment of developing an eight-minute sermon to deliver in class. The only requirement was that they all had to use the same passage and could not collaborate on their sermons. The session when they delivered their sermons was one of the most interesting in which I have ever participated. About fifteen students came up with fifteen quite different sermons on the same text, in spite of using some of the same commentaries in the same college library. The joy of preaching is found in the choices we make about how we approach the biblical text.

You are the interpreter of the text under the guidance of the Holy Spirit. What you see in the text is as unique to you and your congregational life, just as it will be to the next pastor and his or her church situation. Becoming a main character is merely another way of being the interpreter of the text. The joy of preaching as a main character is that you have a myriad of choices, limited only by the insights you find when you are inside the story.

And there are still other ways to accomplish this goal.

STEP 3: MOVING THROUGH THE STORY
BECOMING A MINOR CHARACTER

The temptation in narrative preaching (especially first-person narrative preaching) is to limit yourself to the main character. There is nothing inherently wrong with this, but it is quite limiting. If you are going to undertake narrative preaching to open up new options for your preaching schedule, then limiting yourself to main characters will defeat the very purpose for which you are reading this book. Dealing only with main characters limits you:

1. While there are almost inexhaustible narratives from which you can preach using the main character, you limit the possibility of developing a series of narrative sermons on other texts.

2. Some stories are richer when relayed through the eyes of a minor character than they are through the eyes of the main character.

3. By using only one character, you cannot effectively mine much of the conflict in a biblical story. A second character will have a different take on the same situation.

Remember, conflict usually occurs because two people have differing views on the same subject or situation.

4. As is the case with being the narrator, as a minor character you get to react strongly to what the main character is doing. This gives you an even greater amount of information to convey from the text.

In the story of the prodigal son, you could tell the story from the perspective of the father. How many sermons have you heard that concentrated on the actions and reactions of the father, not the prodigal? In the same way, how many elder brothers do you have sitting in the pews? Or how many people in the congregation relate to the attitudes represented by the elder brother either in their family, on the job, or in the church? Not limiting yourself to the main character can only enhance the richness of this parable. By this, I am not suggesting that you combine multiple characters in one story. (At least I am not suggesting this at the moment. Read on, for there is more to come later.) However, there are several ways to enter the story, and using a minor character may help you formulate your ideas about the text better than just being the main character.

While developing a minor character, use the same types of questions that we utilized in the main character section. Here are some examples from the parable of the prodigal son:

Background questions:

- Father: Where is my wife?

- Father: How differently do I view my two sons? What is my relationship with each of them prior to the loss of the prodigal?

- Father: What has been the relationship between my son and me?

- Elder son: What has been the relationship between my younger brother and me?

- Elder brother: What are my duties and responsibilities on the ranch? What were my brother's responsibilities before he asked for his inheritance and left the farm? How many of his duties did I have to pick up?

Conflict questions:

- Father: Why does my son want to leave the ranch? What have I done to create a situation where he wants to leave the family business?

- Father: Does this take me by surprise, or have I been expecting this moment?

- Elder brother: Why did I not leave and go out on my own? Am I motivated to stay by financial gain, family loyalty, or work ethic?

Questions to flesh out the story:

- Father: How does your faith influence your state of mind when the prodigal does finally return?

- Father/Elder son: What do you do while the prodigal is off in another land?

- Elder son: How does your faith affect your life, considering your reaction to the return of your brother?

Turning-point questions:

- Father: How do you react to your son's demand to give him the inheritance? Should you give it at all? What does the law say about such a request from a younger son? (This question takes you from the turning point of asking for the inheritance and navigates you toward the next turning point, which is his loss of the inheritance.)

- Father: Do you get any reports from anyone concerning your son's actions? If yes, why don't you go and try to persuade your son to leave his life of debauchery and return to the ranch? (This question takes you from the turning point of his son's high living to the job in the pigpen.)

- Elder son: Why do you react in the way you do when your brother returns? What in your values and personality makeup cause you to react so negatively to what your father sees as a very positive event? (This takes you from the prodigal's return to the end of the parable.)

Key-moment questions:

- Father: What emotions do you feel when you see your son coming? (We know his reactions recorded in the text, but does he go through a host of other reactions before deciding to respond in a positive way?)

- Elder brother: What emotions does a faithful son go through when confronted with the amazingly merciful response of your parent to a wayward child? Is your response really as negative as it sounds? Or is it the cry of a wounded son who feels his father does not love him as much as he does the prodigal son?

Resolution questions:

- Father: How do you decide what will be the responsibility of your prodigal son after he returns? Does he come back and have leadership roles? Does he start over as a laborer? How far will you go in restoring your son to the privileges of an heir?

- Elder brother: How far will you go to resolve the break in your relationship with your father and brother? What is the family dynamic at the end of the story? Who is most responsible for this changed dynamic?

By using the same categories of questions, it is possible to develop minor characters in a way that gives fresh insights to the narrative text. After all, one of the strongest arguments for the use of narrative preaching is that it creates a fresh approach to the narrative, both for the preacher and for the listener.

Conclusion

If you are new to narrative preaching, these concepts should enable you to take your first steps. Remember, you do not have to jump into the narrative sermon and suddenly abandon your current methods. You can ease your way into the narrative world. But once you have become comfortable with the ideas of narrator, main character, and minor character, there are some other characters you may choose to develop. If you are ready to move to the next level or are already experienced in narrative preaching, then turn the page and let's move on to even more advanced levels of narrative. You should spend some time practicing and polishing the concepts and techniques of chapter 3, but chapter 4 will give you even more ways in which to engage the text narratively.

4

ADVANCED METHODS IN NARRATIVE PREACHING
USING ANTAGONISTS,
IMPLIED CHARACTERS, AND MULTIPLES

I love to tell the story of unseen things above,
Of Jesus and His glory, of Jesus and His love.

PLAYING THE ANTAGONIST

Most actors will tell you that it is more fun to play the villain than it is to play the hero. The same is true in narrative preaching. If you limit yourself to heroes and positive characters, you omit some powerful insights into many stories in the biblical realm. Telling the story of Elijah from either the perspective of Ahab or (if you dare) Jezebel can bring a quite different slant to this great story of God's faithfulness. If you become Haman in the book of Esther, you can explore the themes of jealousy, hatred, race prejudice, lying, deceit, and destruction. I have a friend in ministry who once told the story of the Gadarene demoniac as the demoniac! (You would have to know Denny to know how incredibly real he can be as a demon-possessed man!)

Plenty of characters whom Scripture portrays negatively make wonderful subjects for narrative sermons (e.g., Herod, the snake in the Garden of Eden, Judas, Sanballat, and Caiaphas).

You should not immediately remove them from your list of acceptable preaching subjects just because they are antagonistic characters; they make great narrative sermons. All the time in our sermons, we use negative examples to contrast with positive ones. We can do the same with negative characters. Here are a few types of antagonistic characters that are rich subjects for narrative preaching:

THE SHAKEN ANTAGONIST

The acts of God shake plenty of biblical characters. At some point in the narrative, these characters have a change of heart and come to embrace all or part of God's truth. Some examples:

> 1. *Pharaoh.* How do the first nine plagues change him? How does the tenth change him? What causes him to change his mind after he lets the Jewish nation go?
>
> 2. *The Philippian jailer.* How does he feel as he goes from repressor to one who embraces the truth?
>
> 3. *The centurion.* Why does he turn from being a dispassionate Roman leader to one who affirms the divine nature of Jesus while watching him on the cross?

THE CONSISTENT ANTAGONIST

Many antagonistic characters in Scripture are constantly nagging the main character. They offer a wealth of possibilities for demonstrating the unfolding story of God's action.

> 1. *Job's three friends* (Eliphaz, Bildad, and Zophar). Each has multiple chapters devoted to his position. Following each man's argument, Job takes a couple of chapters to

reply. These consistently negative characters say things that allow Job to reveal his faith and share his struggle. (Elihu is another antagonistic character in the story.)

2. *The thorn in the flesh.* Not all characters have to be people. Telling the story of Paul's affliction as if you were his thorn has great possibilities.

THE UNREPENTANT ANTAGONIST

These negative characters never repent, never seem shaken by the truth, and never yield to the grace of God.

1. *Ahab and Jezebel.* How could Ahab turn from believing in one God to erecting temples to Baal? What was Jezebel's belief in God, and how did she try to effect change in the nation of Israel?

2. *Ananias and Sapphira.* If either of them had repented, would they have died? What was in their minds as they hatched a plan to fool the church into believing that they were generous givers?

3. *King Saul.* His descent into manic depression and madness destroys his life. Why is he so fearful of the loyal David?

4. *Absalom.* How can a son treat his father as he did? Look through the story of Amnon and Tamar to find some clues.

5. *Judas.* Here's the quintessential unrepentant character. How many times have you tried to discover why he did what he did? Now you can give your interpretation without worrying if it is *the* interpretation.

The antagonist provides a wonderful opportunity to explore how those in sin try to justify their actions. In each case, the antagonist stands in opposition to God, God's servants, and/or God's will. By exposing an antagonist's thought processes and rationalizations, you have opportunity to dispel the kinds of wrong thinking to which many believers still fall prey. If you constantly deal with the hero of a biblical story, you only deal with the successful movements of the spiritual life (with some exceptions). When you deal with the negative characters, you must explore the themes of secularism, power, racism, seduction, pride, unrepentance, and a host of other actions and beliefs that cause human society to fall into the web of sin. These are important themes that you should not ignore if you are to preach the "whole counsel of God" (Acts 20:27 RSV).

DISCOVERING IMPLIED CHARACTERS

Every year, I give a Christmas IQ test to my congregation. It stuns people to realize how much myth they believe and how few facts most churchgoers have accumulated about this nearly universally known biblical story. Here are a few of the questions I ask:

How many wise men came to see Jesus?
a. One
b. Two
c. Three
d. Many
e. None of the above

Who told Mary and Joseph to go to Bethlehem?
a. The angel
b. Mary's mother
c. Herod
d. Caesar Augustus
e. No one

What did the innkeeper tell Mary and Joseph?

a. "There is no room in the inn."

b. "I have a stable you can use."

c. "Come back after the Christmas rush, and I should have some vacancies."

d. Both A and B

e. None of the above

How did you do? For those who are interested, the answer to the first question is *e*: we have no idea how many wise men there were. The number three is widely assumed because they brought three gifts to the Christ child, but the text does not indicate how many wise men there were. The answer to the second question is *d*: the census of Caesar Augustus called them to the town of their ancestral home. The question that really gets them (and gets them every time) is the one about the innkeeper. What did he say? The most common answer is *a*: "There is no room in the inn." Maybe that's your answer. Yet, the gospels of Matthew and Luke do not mention an innkeeper. That's right, no innkeeper! So the correct answer is *e*: None of the above.

Think how many Christmas musicals and plays have the innkeeper as a prominent character in the Christmas story. How do those writers get away with it? The answer is simple. The innkeeper is an implied character. Someone had to tell the couple there was no room at the inn. It could have been any one of a hundred characters, but the easiest and most logical person would have been the innkeeper.

Another implied character familiar to Bible readers is the boy who gave up his lunch at the feeding of the five thousand. Did you know that this feeding is the only miracle during Jesus' public ministry that all four gospels record? Did you also know that in the three Synoptic Gospels, there is no boy? Only in John is the boy mentioned. He never speaks, nor does he even offer his barley loaves and fish. Andrew points out, "Here is a boy" (John 6:8–9), but he does not say that the boy is offering to share his meal, nor does the child speak on his own behalf. But the boy's involvement, his offering of his lunch, his giving of the bread and fish to Jesus—the text implies all of these. Implied characters abound in Scripture.

If you were preaching on the story of the prodigal son, can you think of any characters the story implies but does not state? For instance, would there not have been friends upon whom the prodigal squandered his money? What about the servants at his father's house? How about the pig farmer? In every biblical story or narrative, there are implied characters. And telling the story of the passage from the point of view of an implied character opens up the possibility of seeing the story from yet another point of view.

In the story of Elijah, couldn't you tell the story of the drought from the perspective of an Israelite farmer? I have. In the Christmas story, what would have been the reaction of the lawyer with whom Joseph consulted when he decided to quietly divorce Mary? How about telling the story of Shadrach, Meshach, and Abednego from the perspective of the next soldiers whom the king ordered to stoke the furnace after it had consumed the other soldiers but not the three Hebrews? Telling the story of the crucifixion can take a rather dramatic turn when you become one of the soldiers who nailed Jesus to the cross and gambled for his cloak. The list goes on and on. It is limited only by your own imagination.

During a sermon series on the birth of Christ, I told the Christmas story from the viewpoint of the man in charge of taking the census in Bethlehem. Was there such a character? There must have been. When he met Joseph and they talked together, a very revealing story unfolded. Implied characters require a deeper degree of imagination and a more finely developed sense of character and storytelling. But the seasoned narrative preacher can use them to give a whole new perspective on the story. The text implies so much of what we preach, anyway. The very act of interpretation requires that we constantly make decisions based on what we think the text implies. Again, this is a Spirit-induced process in traditional preaching. In using implied characters in narrative preaching, we should be equally open to the leading of the Spirit as we try to tell the story from the perspective of someone who is implied in the text.

Here is an exercise you might try. Read the following three passages of scripture. They all lend themselves to narrative preaching. In each case, the text describes major and minor characters. Place those characters in two categories (major and minor). Now add the third category of implied characters and see if you can discern any of them in each passage. Here are the passages:

Genesis 39:1–6
Joseph and Potiphar

Now Joseph had been taken down to Egypt. Potiphar, an Egyptian who was one of Pharaoh's officials, the captain of the guard, bought him from the Ishmaelites who had taken him there.

The LORD was with Joseph and he prospered, and he lived in the house of his Egyptian master. When his master saw that the LORD was with him and that the LORD gave him success in everything he did, Joseph found favor in his eyes and became his attendant. Potiphar put him in charge of his household, and he entrusted to his care everything he owned. From the time he put him in charge of his household and of all that he owned, the LORD blessed the household of the Egyptian because of Joseph. The blessing of the LORD was on everything Potiphar had, both in the house and in the field. So he left in Joseph's care everything he had; with Joseph in charge, he did not concern himself with anything except the food he ate.

Acts 13:1–12
Barnabas and Saul Sent Off

¹In the church at Antioch there were prophets and teachers: Barnabas, Simeon called Niger, Lucius of Cyrene, Manaen (who had been brought up with Herod the tetrarch) and Saul. ²While they were worshiping the Lord and fasting, the Holy Spirit said, "Set apart for me Barnabas and Saul for the work to which I have called them." ³So after they had fasted and prayed, they placed their hands on them and sent them off.

⁴The two of them, sent on their way by the Holy Spirit, went down to Seleucia and sailed from there to Cyprus. ⁵When they arrived at Salamis, they proclaimed the word of God in the Jewish synagogues. John was with them as their helper.

⁶They traveled through the whole island until they came to Paphos. There they met a Jewish sorcerer and false prophet named Bar-Jesus, ⁷who was an attendant of the

proconsul, Sergius Paulus. The proconsul, an intelligent man, sent for Barnabas and Saul because he wanted to hear the word of God. [8]But Elymas the sorcerer (for that is what his name means) opposed them and tried to turn the proconsul from the faith. [9]Then Saul, who was also called Paul, filled with the Holy Spirit, looked straight at Elymas and said, [10]"You are a child of the devil and an enemy of everything that is right! You are full of all kinds of deceit and trickery. Will you never stop perverting the right ways of the Lord? [11]Now the hand of the Lord is against you. You are going to be blind, and for a time you will be unable to see the light of the sun."

Immediately mist and darkness came over him, and he groped about, seeking someone to lead him by the hand. [12]When the proconsul saw what had happened, he believed, for he was amazed at the teaching about the Lord.

Luke 1:5–22
The Birth of John the Baptist Foretold

In the time of Herod king of Judea there was a priest named Zechariah, who belonged to the priestly division of Abijah; his wife Elizabeth was also a descendant of Aaron. Both of them were upright in the sight of God, observing all the Lord's commandments and regulations blamelessly. But they had no children, because Elizabeth was barren; and they were both well along in years.

Once when Zechariah's division was on duty and he was serving as priest before God, he was chosen by lot, according to the custom of the priesthood, to go into the temple of the Lord and burn incense. And when the time for the burning of incense came, all the assembled worshipers were praying outside.

Then an angel of the Lord appeared to him, standing at the right side of the altar of incense. When Zechariah saw him, he was startled and was gripped with fear. [13]But the angel said to him: "Do not be afraid, Zechariah; your prayer has been heard. Your wife Elizabeth will bear you a son, and you are to give him the name John. He will be a joy and delight to you, and many will rejoice because of his birth, for he will be great in the sight of the Lord. He is never to take wine or other fermented drink, and he will be filled with the Holy Spirit even from birth. Many of the people of Israel will he bring back to the Lord their God. And he will go on before the Lord, in the spirit and power of Elijah, to turn the hearts of the fathers to their children and the disobedient to the wisdom of the righteous—to make ready a people prepared for the Lord."

Zechariah asked the angel, "How can I be sure of this? I am an old man and my wife is well along in years."

The angel answered, "I am Gabriel. I stand in the presence of God, and I have been sent to speak to you and to tell you this good news. And now you will be silent and not able to speak until the day this happens, because you did not believe my words, which will come true at their proper time."

Meanwhile, the people were waiting for Zechariah and wondering why he stayed so long in the temple. When he came out, he could not speak to them. They realized he had seen a vision in the temple, for he kept making signs to them but remained unable to speak.

Well, how did you do? There are certainly several implied characters in each passage above. Were you able to find more than one? More than five? Even more than that? It would be interesting to tell the story of Joseph from the perspective of the Ishmaelite leader who sold him to Potiphar. So would telling about Joseph's success from the viewpoint of a servant in Potiphar's field or of an Egyptian businessman who dealt with Joseph as he managed the house. In the story of Paul's first journey, did you think about Paul and Barnabas telling the ship's captain (or the sailors on board) about their call and the gospel story? Imagine telling Elymas's story from the perspective of the man who took him by the hand to lead him after he was struck blind. In the last scripture selection, what about being one of the priests who got the short straw? Or the worshipers who came to offer prayers that day? (You could tell the story either from the perspective of being there when Zechariah entered the temple or from the perspective of seeing him when he came out.) You probably have more characters on your list than I have suggested here. That is the fascination of telling a biblical story from an implied character's standpoint.

Handling Multiple Characters in the Same Sermon

One of the more advanced ideas in narrative preaching is to handle multiple characters in the same message. Obviously, this requires some skill, not only in developing characters, but also in portraying them. There are some unique advantages to this method:

1. Instead of having to choose between major and minor characters, you can portray both in the same sermon. For instance, you can be all three of the main characters

in the prodigal son parable (son, father, and elder brother). In the above examples, you could be both Joseph and Potiphar, or Paul and Sergius Paulus, or Zechariah and Gabriel.

2. Telling the story from multiple perspectives allows you to create some dialogue between differing characters. While a real dialogue would require more than one person, shifting your narrative between different characters could allow you to suggest some back-and-forth debate.

How one uses multiple characters in a narrative sermon requires an extra measure of creativity. There are, however, some quite powerful ways in which this can be done. Here are a few suggestions:

1. If you have a multiple staff or some creative people in your church, use more than one person in the sermon. Let each speaker develop the sermon from the viewpoint of the character they choose. Be sure to find ways to make the transitions between the speakers.

2. Use the role of the narrator to introduce each of the characters. If you do this, have different places on the platform where you stand when you are that character. (You don't have to exaggerate this. Just make sure you are always to the left of center when you are one character and to the right of center when you are another; this will help the congregation follow your transitions and dialogue.) The narrator can transition to a new character by saying something like this: "Here is what the father thought when his prodigal son left home . . ."

3. As a variation of suggestion 2, write out a script for the narrator and give that role to someone else in the church. This will not take a great deal of work on either of your parts, but it can make an effective visual tool for transitioning between characters. As long as you can give a prearranged signal or cue for the narrator to read the prepared text (it can be as simple as your moving away from your spot or sitting down when finished with one character), you should be able to make the transitions smoothly.

4. A third variation on this theme is to have someone read the role of the narrator as it is in the biblical text. When the narrator gets to the point where the text introduces the first main character, you can begin to portray and tell that character's story. For instance, when preaching on Acts 13, you could have the narrator read the first seven verses. As the narrator finishes, tell that part of the story from the perspective of either Paul or Barnabas. Then have the narrator return and read verses 8–11a. At that point, you become the character of Elymas and make your case against the missionaries. Following that, have the narrator pick up again with verses 11b–12, and you can finish the sermon by speaking as the proconsul who comes to believe.

5. If you know other preachers in your community who are exploring narrative sermons, partner with them and have a unity service where several of you speak as multiple characters from a biblical text. If you don't know of any other preachers doing this, bring it up at a ministerial meeting and see if anyone is interested.

6. Preach the sermon in several sections, each at a different time in the worship service. For instance, when preaching the story of the prodigal son, you could portray the younger son in the early part of the service, the father in the middle of the service, and the elder brother toward the end of the service. Placing other elements of worship between the sermon stories makes a clear demarcation between the characters and creates fresh anticipation each time you get up to portray another aspect of the narrative from the mind of a different character.

CONCLUSION

As with any sermon, when using multiple characters, you must be aware of the time this requires. Developing a character story usually makes the sermon a bit shorter than most other forms of preaching (as least that has been true with those who are new to the process). The laypeople may well be excited to hear that you will be preaching shorter sermons, We preachers, though, must understand that what matters is not how long we preach but how much we say. However, when you begin using multiple characters in a sermon, it is quite possible that the total sermon time will run longer than necessary. Pare down each character's story so that your presentation is still effective and memorable.

5

WHEN THE NARRATIVE CEASES
PREACHING OUT OF THE BOX WITHOUT GETTING OUT OF THE TEXT

I love to tell the story— for some have never heard
The message of salvation from God's own holy word.

PICTURING WHAT CANNOT BE PICTURED

I recently attended my first service at Willow Creek Community Church in the Chicago suburbs. As we approached the entry doors to the church, I noticed that several of them were draped with the yellow tape that surrounds areas under construction or indicating danger. I assumed that they were having some construction done on part of the building, so these doors were not in use. I could not have been more wrong.

As we got closer to the doors, I noticed that the yellow tape had the words "Identity Theft" on it. On the building was a warning about the need for spiritual construction on the soul. As we entered the lobby area, we saw a caricature hanging from beams, balconies, and walls. This character was in profile, completely black in color with the exception of a slightly lighter mask that covered the area of face around an eye. (The eye itself was exposed.) He had the look of a thief. By then, all the symbols came into focus. Here was the identity thief who had stolen our true identities. It wasn't too much of an imaginative stretch to see in his appearance the character of Satan. Before I entered the sanctuary, I had a picture of what the general theme for the service and for the message would be. I soon learned this was the title of a sermon series that was being preached and that there was an even more specific title for the sermon that day.

At the rear of the auditorium, an usher handed us the bulletin for the day. The same caricature and yellow "Identity Thief" tape appeared on the front of the bulletin. Also on the front of the bulletin was the title of the day's sermon by teaching pastor Mike Breaux: "Mugged by the Mirror." During the message, Pastor Breaux told the story of Adam and Eve in the Garden of Eden and made the powerful application of how Satan has stolen our true identity as children of God. On the platform, slightly behind where Breaux was sitting during the sharing of the sermon, were two full-length mirrors hung side by side. As he told the story of Satan's destruction of our innocence, Breaux picked up an apple from a table, wheeled about, and threw it at one of the mirrors. The apple shattered the glass, destroying his reflected image. The apple then rolled across the stage for several yards. You could have heard a pin drop among the ten thousand members of the congregation. The people saw Satan's theft of our true identities—suggested by the crime-scene tape, banner caricatures, and bulletin covers—now openly portrayed in the shattered mirror and the rolling apple. It was as if we were in the garden itself, seeing the theft through the eyes of heavenly witnesses.

If I asked you to picture identity theft as a concept, what image would have come to mind? Those of us in the audience that Sunday will never again wonder how to picture the concept of Satan destroying our God-ordained identities. Our minds will always conjure up the image of a mirror broken by an apple. We had seen what, before the sermon, we could not have imagined.

In the Lucas Learning System, Jerry Lucas has taken this same principle and applied it to our learning process. After showing you a picture of a nun swinging a golf club, he writes: "You see an obvious picture of a nun. She is swinging a golf club. She is a very good golfer. In fact, she is a pro golfer. That makes her a *pro-nun* or a *pronoun*. Now you have seen your first pronoun."[1] When I attended Dr. Lucas's lectures and was confronted with the picture of a "pro-nun" (pronoun), I was in full agreement. I had never seen a picture of a pronoun. Once he had enabled me to picture what I assumed could not be pictured, I found myself seeing many other unimaginable things. This is the work of a storyteller.

To be a narrative preacher, to believe in storytelling as a valid way of sharing the gospel, you must believe that you can picture what cannot be pictured. Narrative preachers *see* a sermon because storytelling happens in pictures, not words. To picture what cannot be imagined releases to the listener's minds a vehicle through which they can participate in the story. When we preach propositional truths, we often project concepts on a screen and ask our listeners to remember these points. In narrative preaching, we put a picture in front of our listeners and ask them to see the story—even to see what they think cannot be seen and picture what they think cannot be pictured.

RENARRATING THE TEXT

As a rule, a storyteller does not need a narrative to tell a story. All you need is an idea, concept, or concern. During

---

1. Lucas, *Learning How to Learn*, 39. In fairness to Lucas's system, he does this as a part of his "sound-alike word system." The principle is one he applies in many different styles of his memory systems.

a pastors conference at Moody Bible Institute a few years ago, a friend of mine attended a service where the speaker came out on the platform to preach a sermon based on 1 Corinthians 3:1–3:

> [1]Brothers, I could not address you as spiritual but as worldly—mere infants in Christ. [2]I gave you milk, not solid food, for you were not yet ready for it. Indeed, you are still not ready. [3]You are still worldly. For since there is jealousy and quarreling among you, are you not worldly? Are you not acting like mere men?

This is not a passage most preachers would use as the basis for a narrative sermon. Where's the narrative? Those of us trained in propositional preaching might try to figure out how to illustrate what Paul says. We might pick up a gallon of milk and a plate of dinner food to demonstrate the difference between milk and solid food. We might go to the Internet and gather facts and figures concerning the dietary needs of people as they relate to just drinking milk versus eating solid food. Most of us would undoubtedly talk about how an infant moves from a diet of mother's milk to the solid food of the dinner table as a way of indicating growth and maturity. All are good suggestions, but none of them are narrative preaching. What do you think the speaker did?

The speaker walked onto the platform dressed in a diaper with a massive pacifier hanging around his neck. As the shocked audience of preachers reacted to this, the speaker began his sermon with these words: "I'm a baby Christian, and I'm you're worst nightmare." Do you think he had their attention? Further along, he grasped the pacifier hanging around his neck and asked, "You know what my biggest problem is?

It's this. Eternal security!" I can guarantee that those listening to the sermon were picturing these concepts for the first time.

Preaching narrative sermons from nonnarrative passages is an effective way of sharing grand theological ideas in conceptual ways. The problem is not that such passages lack narrative material but that we have not allowed our study to bring out the marvelous stories encased in nonnarrative passages.

For instance, in the passage quoted above from 1 Corinthians, we find the real significance of the epistle in background information that we come to know through reading Bible commentaries and other survey materials. Such information helps us to know the situation in Corinth that prompted the writing. Because there were grave problems in the Corinthian church, Paul wrote several letters expressing his dismay, appreciation, and concern for the people of the church. Knowing this information gives you a narrative milieu from which to approach the text. William Willimon says that this is the great task of preachers.

> Our great challenge, as epistolary preachers, is to renarrate Paul's letters. I assume that every Pauline letter arises from some congregational story...In order to preach a letter, every preacher, even non-narrative preachers, must construct, reconstruct, and imaginatively re-create the story and deliver it in some sort of dynamic equivalent to the biblical text in order to do what the text does.[2]

I believe that Willimon has expressed the challenge in perfect terms for anyone who seeks to do narrative preaching from nonnarrative texts: We must renarrate the story.

---

2. Willimon, "Preaching the Letters as Narrative," 107.

TOOLS FOR RENARRATING A TEXT

To renarrate a biblical text, the preacher must know several things. None of these will seem new to anyone who is a serious student of preaching. However, they are important enough to review.

BACKGROUND INFORMATION

In our hurry to do biblical exegesis for sermons, pastors often skip the introductory sections of commentaries and survey books. Yet these sections describe the context of the book, which often affects the original writing and our interpretation of the text. No biblical book arrives in a vacuum. Every book comes to us in the context of a story. All of Paul's epistles have a historical context that we should know. First John has a definite group of people whom John desires to warn about the theological controversies of the day (Gnosticism). According to most scholars, the physical brothers of Jesus wrote James and Jude. And what if Hebrews was written by Priscilla rather than a man? Such background material will inform any preacher. To the narrative preacher, this is a wealth of story-driven material that can help to renarrate these nonnarrative books.

Consider the book of Acts. While Acts is a wonderful narrative book in itself, it also gives us the context of many of the letters of Paul. The background and story of the events of the church to which Paul writes epistles are often found in Acts. Let me give you a couple of examples of narrative background that creates the story of Paul's letters:

The beginning of the church in Thessalonica is found in Acts 17:1–9. It is a story of Paul and his entourage planting an infant church in the local Jewish synagogue. Joined by factions of "God-fearing Greeks," this church plant was challenged almost immediately by a Jewish-led riot against them.

Paul and his company fled for their lives, and the person hosting them (Jason) was dragged before the city officials, where he was accused of treason and required to post bond. Needless to say, this is a life-or-death challenge to the new church, especially since it was without mature leadership after Paul and the evangelistic team had escaped. This in itself is a powerful narrative story.

However, when you read 1 Thessalonians 2:17–3:13, you get the rest of the story. Here Paul tells of his emotions at having to leave the young church. He describes how he sent Timothy to find out what has happened following the mob scene. And he shares his elation at the encouraging report brought back to him by Timothy. Nearly the whole of 1 Thessalonians is a reaction to the events related in Acts and the subsequent trip and report from Timothy. When Paul takes up the theme of living "to please God" in chapter 4, he describes sanctification and holiness as a result of the Thessalonians' faithfulness to God during persecution. Paul states his unyielding belief that those who are consecrated by fire are holy in the eyes of the Lord. Propositional preaching may pick up the same theme, but only a renarration of the text enables you to communicate the power of the story. The story makes your preaching on obedience and sanctification far more real to the listener than a mere reciting of intellectual concepts.

In the book of Acts, we first meet Timothy (16:1) and see him as he begins his traveling missions work with Paul and Silas (16:3). In Acts 19–20, Luke tells in some detail of the work in Ephesus. Paul finds a spiritually immature group of believers there and takes two years to bring them up to a more mature level of believing. During this time, Timothy joins him and becomes part of the teaching team. Eventually, a riot breaks out against Paul and his teachings. He flees to Macedonia and then to Troas, before finally sending for the Ephesian elders, to give them farewell instructions.

Paul's First Letter to Timothy begins with a warning against false teachers. Paul writes, "As I urged you when I went into Macedonia, stay there in Ephesus so that you may command certain men not to teach false doctrines any longer nor to devote themselves to myths and endless genealogies. These promote controversies rather than God's work—which is by faith" (1 Tim 1:3–4). When you renarrate the text of 1 Timothy, you find that Paul's teaching about the role of Timothy in ferreting out false teachers arises from the story of Ephesus and the two-year ministry that Paul had there. Suddenly, the admonition against false teachers has a context and Timothy has a life situation into which he interprets the words of his mentor. This information is valuable for propositional preaching. In narrative preaching, it becomes a background against which Timothy must confront the false teachers or they will be left to persuade and prevail. It is also possible that you could go from 1 Timothy into the Letter to the Ephesians and find parallel material, which will further highlight the story and provide a narrative understanding of that text. With this information at your disposal, what was nonnarrative material now becomes the subject of narrative preaching.

WRITER/READER PERSPECTIVE

You can renarrate a text by sharing the story from the perspective of either the writer or the original reader. For instance, Paul writes his letter to the Colossians from prison. Placing a Colossian text in the midst of imprisonment gives a story context to renarrate. You could give Paul's view as he writes from his prison cell (or house arrest, as the case may be) and show how that confinement informs what Paul writes. On the other hand, listeners could receive another wealth of narrative material through hearing a Colossian believer tell how this new letter has arrived and how eager they are to hear from their founder, apostle, and hero in faith. Discovering the meaning of what Paul writes can be a marvelous way of exegeting a passage in a narrative sermon form. Here are some other nonnarrative books that have incredibly rich narrative possibilities, especially when done from the writer/reader perspective:

Psalms. Many of the psalms give you their historical context.[3] Sometimes the preamble to the psalm supplies this. More than telling you what instrument or time signature you should use, these introductory words may give you historical detail or setting you can use narratively.

For example, read Psalm 3 and its superscription. David's being betrayed by his son Absalom is a compelling narrative story. Adding this story's emotions and feelings to the thoughts and theology of Psalm 3 makes it even more powerful. Psalm 3 enables you to interject into the story the words and inner thoughts of a king and father who is betrayed by his son and heir. Another example is Psalm 30, which indicates that it was written for the dedication service of the temple. Using it in conjunction with the temple dedication story or even the story of how Solomon finally built

---

3. Books like Anderson's *Out of the Depths* are invaluable tools for finding the historical and thematic construction of the book of Psalms. It gives many divisions of the types of psalms that are in the book as well as supplying historical contextualization to those divisions, thus opening up innumerable narrative possibilities.

the temple could be a most interesting narrative story, using a nonnarrative text.

Look at Psalms 120–134. The superscriptions identify them all as "songs of ascents." In other words, pilgrims sang these songs as they made their way up to the city of Jerusalem and to the temple mount. Imagine a visitor, perhaps someone in the later years of life who is coming to the temple for the first time. A lifelong dream is about to be realized. As he approaches the city, the pilgrims around him begin to sing, "How good and pleasant it is when brothers live together in unity!" (Ps 133:1). The unbridled joy of worshiping the Lord and worshiping in community flows out of this scene. It is ripe for a narrative treatment.

Proverbs. Most of the proverbs in this book have a picture quality to them. While experienced narrative preachers may be able to build an entire narrative sermon on a single proverb, it is more likely that one will need a larger group of proverbial statements to fill out a sermon. You might use a larger text that has a more concentrated thought, or you might follow the threads of cross-reference found in most study Bibles to similar passages elsewhere in the biblical text.

For example, beginning in Proverbs 1:8 and recurring at the beginning of chapters 2 through 7, the writer gives a series of addresses on the value of wisdom. In each case a father speaks the lesson to a son and recalls valuable lessons that the father has learned. Imagine a series of sermons done narratively on teaching spiritual values to our children. One Sunday you could have an infant in a crib on stage (real or a doll, depending on the depth of your faith or your ability to put children to sleep). On successive Sundays, you could put older children on stage until you have a final sermon with either a teenaged son or even a young adult male. You could even make this sermon a dialogue with the young man, if it seems appropriate.

Since nearly all proverbs are pictorial in nature, they are snapshots of wisdom. "The wise woman builds her house, but with her own hands the foolish one tears hers down" (Prov 14:1). This is a powerful text for a sermon on domestic violence or child abuse. On a stage littered with debris from a house in disarray, the musings of a husband about his wife's problems or a first-person narrative of a woman who has thrown away her life would be powerful. Maybe you could have someone from the congregation who has experienced the destruction of her life by her own hand (drugs, alcohol, infidelity) start your sermon by sharing her testimony. Your sermon could then be the story of picking up the strewn pieces of debris on the stage and putting life back together.

If you own a *Thompson Chain-Reference Bible*, you can easily follow the chains of ideas that pop up throughout the book of Proverbs. Themes of true wisdom, knowledge, uprightness, discretion, and many others run throughout the book of Proverbs. As with any sermon, finding a theme gives you an organizing perspective. However, in narrative preaching, there are times when you also embody the theme. In other words, you *become* true wisdom or knowledge or discretion, and you address the congregation as that virtue. You can also use this treatment for other proverbial statements found in both the Old and New Testaments.

Revelation. With its picturesque language and otherworldly setting, Revelation lends itself well to a narrative approach, even when the examples cited are more complicated than a normal story may require. There are bowls of wrath, seals being broken, scrolls being opened, living creatures, lambs, and horsemen riding on colored horses—all of which lend themselves to the narrative experience. You need little renarration when preaching from the book of Revelation, but you may have to do some recontextualization to apply the meaning of the passage to your listeners.

While presenting God's message to the seven churches, you could become the angel who writes these words to each church or become a member of one of the churches (even its pastor). Such treatments would be easy adaptations of the writer/reader concept. You could also become the writer of the book, John the Revelator, rather than an angel to the church. There are so many characters in the book, real and fanciful, that you could tell the story of these events from the perspective of any number of them. Take your pick: four living creatures, one of the 144,000, one of the multitude standing before the throne in white robes, and others.

ABSTRACT CONCRETENESS

To truly translate nonnarrative passages into narrative sermons requires some imagineering, as described earlier in the book. Like the preacher who translated Paul's teachings about spiritual maturity into a character who says, "I'm a baby Christian, and I'm your worst nightmare," the narrative task requires the preacher to take something abstract and make it more concrete. This imaginative process works somewhat like the parables of the Synoptics. Jesus had a concept he desired his followers to understand. To accomplish his teaching goal, he created a story context to teach the main point of the message. In other words, Jesus took an abstract concept (forgiveness) and put it into a concrete process (the parable of the prodigal son). In the case of narrative preaching, the speaker also must take an abstract concept (a nonnarrative passage) and put it into a more concrete story form. Preachers are used to taking a biblical parable and breaking it down into abstract ideas that form the points of a sermon. If you can reverse that process by taking the abstract ideas of a nonnarrative passage and putting them into a story form, then you have created what I call abstract concreteness. Here are a few exercises with possible solutions that may help you practice this activity.

Concept 1

Read the passage below and see if you can convert it into a narrative sermon by using the principle of abstract concreteness:

> Who shall separate us from the love of Christ? Shall trouble or hardship or persecution or famine or nakedness or danger or sword?...No, in all these things we are more than conquerors through him who loved us. For I am convinced that neither death nor life, neither angels nor demons, neither the present nor the future, nor any powers, neither height nor depth, nor anything else in all creation will be able to separate us from the love of God that is in Christ Jesus our Lord. (Rom 8:35, 37–39)

How could you express these rather concrete concepts in story form or in a parable-like process? Stop reading at this point, take out some paper and a pen, and begin writing down your ideas. Then compare your ideas with the ones given below. This is not a test but an exercise in creative thinking. The ideas below are just that—ideas. Yours have just as much validity as mine do. Be creative. (Follow the same procedure after every "Concept" subheading. Don't go on until you have put down some creative ideas of your own. By the time you get to the final three "Concept" sections, you shouldn't need any more prompting from the author. Just write down your ideas and follow your sanctified imagination.)

Idea 1. Pick up on the concept that "we are more than conquerors" and present yourself as an army general giving marching orders to the troops (like General George Patton in the opening scene of the movie *Patton* [1970]).

Idea 2. Tell a real-life story of someone who has gone through any of the trials described in verse 35. As a variation on the theme, bring in several people who have gone through difficult times and let them share their stories. After they tell their stories (or after one person gives a testimony), you can become the voice of God, giving assurance to the congregation that you will never leave them nor forsake them.

Idea 3. Get a helium-filled balloon with the word *love* on it. (I'm sure you can find this at a florist shop or hospital gift shop.) Attach the balloon to your belt and behind your back. Make sure the string on the balloon is long enough so that the balloon will be visibly floating above your head as you preach. As you detail each problem listed in the text, problems that people think separate them from the love of God, you could ask, "Where is the love of God?" This is most effective when the speaker is able to move around the platform or even walk along the center aisle. How you choose to resolve that question will give you a wonderful conclusion to the sermon and a unique ending for your worship service.

Concept 2

In 1 Corinthians 14, Paul details some concrete teaching about speaking in tongues and prophecy. Read over the first 25 verses and observe the debate Paul has concerning this issue of worship. How would you make the concrete concepts of propriety in the Christian worship experience real to a twenty-first-century audience?

> *Idea 1.* Be a first-time visitor at the Corinthian church and describe what it is like to be a nonbeliever in a church that speaks in tongues but doesn't preach the gospel in a language you can understand. Describe the meeting's apparent disorder and confusion as you listen to unintelligible tongues and fail to understand the gospel message. At the end, walk out of the service, wishing aloud that you understood the purpose of this gathering.

> *Idea 2.* If you speak a foreign language fluently, read the text and then preach on it in a language unfamiliar to the congregation. If you do not know another language, invite someone who does to preach a sermon for you, without a translator. In either case, preach the sermon without comment. Make sure it is brief but not too brief (maybe half the normal time of one of your sermons). Following the sermon, have your worship leader sing a closing song and ask all who wish to respond to the sermon to stand or come forward. Then go back to the pulpit, reread the text, and preach the same sermon in English (or the native tongue of the congregation). Make sure both sermons say the same thing, in case someone in the congregation actually speaks the foreign language you've chosen. At the end of the second sermon, call for another hymn and ask all who now wish

to respond to stand or come forward. You can conclude by pointing out that whatever we say and do in worship should be understandable to everyone, including those who do not yet know or grasp the gospel.

Idea 3. Based on the phrase in verse 25 ("secrets of the . . . heart" [NRSV]), you could do a monologue while pulling slips of paper with "secrets" from inside your coat pocket or from a poster-board heart that you have on the platform. Choose to reveal secrets that might inspire someone to bow down and worship God (v. 25).

Concept 3

In 1 Corinthians 12, Paul describes the gifts of the Spirit. How would you renarrate the text?

Idea 1. Play the part of a gift-giver, handing out boxes of spiritual gifts to the congregation. Describe the spiritual gift that is in each box, and then hand it to a person who already expresses that particular gift.

Idea 2. Demonstrate the truth of verse 12: "The body is a unit, though it is made up of many parts; and though all its parts are many, they form one body. So it is with Christ." From a local department store borrow a mannequin that can be dismantled in part or in whole. Picking up each limb or body section, attach it to the main frame of the body. As you do, describe the function of that body part. For instance, pick up the hand and attach it to the arm, while talking about the function of a hand and explaining how the hand serves the needs of the whole body. As you build the mannequin, you will also be building your narrative.

Concept 4

How could you express the attitude of Christ as described in Philippians 2:1–11?

> *Idea 1.* In your preaching, act out what it means to be a servant, such as washing someone's feet, having someone hurl insults at you and receiving them with humility and love, and so on. You could choose other characteristics of Christlike attitudes, such as humility, like-mindedness, or being one in spirit and purpose, and then find ways to demonstrate them in the midst of the congregation.

Concept 5

How can you make the book of Proverbs come alive? The book is full of characters, so the easiest way to narrate a lesson from this book is to become a character.

> *Idea 1.* Be a virtuous woman or someone searching for one. Use the text of Proverbs 31:10–31 as your source of information.

> *Idea 2.* Take any image from Proverbs (it is rich in imagery) and become that object or image. Be the rod (and don't spoil the child!). The rod of discipline is a common theme in several proverbs. Being an inanimate object is one of the opportunities you have in narrative preaching that you really can't do in methodological preaching.

Concept 6

Do a ten-part series on the Beatitudes. You could be a person in the crowd who has the quality about which Jesus is preaching. Give your reaction to the Savior singling you out or promising you incredible things.

Concept 7

Be one of the holy utensils in the tabernacle. What does it mean to be used only in the service of God? How does it feel to be the vessel that others use to worship God? What are you sacrificing to be a holy vessel?

Concept 8

Be the tablet upon which God writes the Ten Commandments. Describe the touch of God's finger upon you. Describe your first view of the nation in sin as Moses brings you off the mountain, and so on.

CREATING YOUR OWN PARABLES

Most preachers who take on the challenge of narrative preaching rely exclusively on narrative Scripture passages. But it is not the exclusive realm of narrative preaching. If you choose to venture into nonnarrative passages, you may find the opportunity to create your own parables. This is not sacrilegious. Parables have been around a long time, long before New Testament times. In cultures which use storytelling as their primary method of sharing history and tradition, parable stories have always existed.[4] Jesus will not be offended if you employ the same method that he used in order to share the truths of God. He will delight in your parables just as surely as God delighted in his Son's parables.

Since modern storytellers are not well-versed in creating parables, it might be good to remind ourselves that this is a process to be learned rather than a supernatural gift that one suddenly receives from above. Let's review the steps:

---

4. Bewer, *Literature of the Old Testament*, 60–61.

First, renarrate a text by using background material. This is the best way to start, and it is the easiest way to approach the epistles of Paul. With Acts as your background, you have plenty of contexts to share. If you have been doing narrative messages from narrative sections, this will seem the most natural way to do narrative preaching. Once you have done a few of these, move on to stage two.

Second, use the Psalms as the concluding illustration of your narrative sermon rather than trying to narrate a specific Psalm. In other words, tell the narrative story from the historical books (Samuel, Kings, Chronicles) and use the Psalms as the concluding reference. One of the earliest narrative sermons I ever did was about Psalm 3. I told the story of the conflict between David and Absalom and how it had developed. It is a gripping narrative. In closing, I left my hearers with the image of a grieving father betrayed by his own son, struggling to know how to react to the events. Was this God's will? Was it punishment for David's sins? What did this startling turn of events really mean? And then I said, "Maybe now you can more fully understand the mind and heart of David when he writes the Third Psalm." Then I read the psalm as the conclusion of the sermon. It is a quite effective way of renarrating a passage.

Third, when you become more comfortable with renarrating a scriptural concept, try taking an inanimate object or a theological concept and bringing it to life. It takes far more advanced skill, but it can reenergize your listeners as well as you. This chapter has given you some examples and some questions to help you creatively renarrate a text that most preachers would never consider narratively. In the process, you will discover the amazing process of creating your own parables. When you do, you are moving closer to the teaching style of Jesus than you may think.

CONCLUSION

Once upon a time, Truth went about the streets as naked as the day he was born. As a result, no one would let him into their homes. Whenever people caught sight of him, they turned away and fled. One day when Truth was sadly wandering about, he came upon Parable. Now Parable was dressed in splendid clothes of beautiful colors. And Parable, seeing Truth, said, "Tell me, neighbor, what makes you look so sad?"

Truth replied bitterly, "Ah, brother, things are bad. Very bad. I'm old, very old, and no one wants to acknowledge me. No one wants anything to do with me."

Hearing that, Parable said, "People don't run away from you because you're old. I too am old. Very old. But the older I get, the better people like me. I'll tell you a secret: Everyone likes things dressed up a bit. Let me lend you some splendid clothes like mine, and you'll see that the very people who pushed you aside will invite you into their homes and be glad of your company."

Truth took Parable's advice and put on the borrowed clothes. And from that time on, Truth and Parable have gone hand-in-hand together and everyone loves them. They make a happy pair.[5]

This is what a storyteller does. This is the underlying foundation of creating your own parables. You take truth and dress it up so that those of a new generation will see truth in a new light.

---

5. Weinreich, *Yiddish Folktales.*

6

FOCUS IN THE SERMON
HOW TO MAKE A REALLY GOOD
VEGETABLE STEW

I love to tell the story— more wonderful it seems
Than all the golden fancies of all our golden dreams.

CITY SLICKER THEOLOGY

Billy Crystal and Jack Palance had an unforgettable conversation in the movie *City Slickers* (1991) that has worked its way into modern vernacular. Palance, the old crusty cowboy of days gone by, tells Crystal, a city slicker on a pretend cattle drive, that his problem is that he doesn't know what the secret of life really is. Eager to find out the meaning of life, Crystal begs Palance to tell him what the meaning of life is. Palance then holds up one finger and says that the secret to life is this (one finger). Crystal is baffled and doesn't understand what he means. Palance tells him that's for Crystal to find out. By the end of the movie, Crystal has figured out that the secret of life is finding that one thing you love to do and doing it well.

I'm not sure how well the scene holds up to theological scrutiny, but I do know that Palance had a valid point when it comes to narrative preaching. To tell an effective story, you have to home in on one thing and tell it well. The story has to have a central theme, a recurring perspective to hold it together. This is also true of nonnarrative-based sermons, but I see little evidence of this in most preaching of any type. Propositional sermons have a tendency to be three points that often do not even relate to one another or barely to the text. My mentor in college was Dr. Marie Strong, who used to tell us that a three-point sermon was supposed to have a first point, which was the main point of the passage; then it was to have a second point, which restated the first; and finally, it was to have a third point which again was to restate the first point in another way. If one followed this advice, the three-point sermon would have at least one good point! To say it another way, make sure that your main point is the main point. What we desperately need in the pulpit is a city slicker theology that keeps us focused on the main point, the one thing that makes a sermon or a story gripping.

In narrative preaching, a story is supposed to have a main point, an overall thrust that you find yourself returning to again and again. John Walsh believes that an effective storyteller goes through a fourteen-step process. Step 5 is to "Establish the Story's One Central Theme." He writes, "Storytellers often make one of two mistakes: either the story is devoid of any theme, or it is overloaded with lessons. The first step in making a story unforgettable is to establish one central truth in the story."[1] This may be the most important revelation that can occur to most storytellers. Simplicity works best. In order to tell what Walsh calls an "unforgettable story," you have to realize that the power of story is in its simplicity of message.

---

1. Walsh, *Art of Storytelling*, 46.

My wife and I often watch movies, either at the theater or on DVD. The more complicated the plot, the more time we spend talking to one another in an effort to keep the plot line and characters straight. Sometimes, we take more time trying to connect the dots in our minds than we do enjoying the movie. My wife is famous for leaning over and asking, "Now, who is that guy again?" or, "What does that mean?" It is distracting for both of us. Either we cannot understand what the director is doing, or we cannot comprehend what the screenwriter's point is. It may work well for a novel to have many plot lines that eventually resolve in the end, but it is death for a storyteller to try to tell too many tales in one story. The effectiveness of the story is diminished by its complexity. Some screenwriters might disagree with me when it comes to movies, but I believe that this is definitely true when it comes to narrative sermonic development. Less is more when telling the plot of a story.

JESUS AND THE KISS METHOD

Jesus followed a tried-and-true method for telling stories. He used the KISS method (Keep It Simple, Savior). Each of his parables told a single story rather than a complex collection of stories. With great simplicity, the good Samaritan parable (Luke 10:25–37) tells the plight of a robbery victim and the reactions of a Levite and a priest as they pass by. Even in relating the reaction of the Good Samaritan, he moves quickly through the story. Why? Simply put, Jesus has a point he is trying to make. And to Jesus, the main point is the main thing. The story is intended to facilitate his hearers' understanding of the point. A parable is not a novel. Jesus uses this method because it gives him a vehicle to arrive at his destination with some speed. Preachers often suffer from the mistaken idea that they should focus on several sermon *points* rather than let the sermon *point* toward the theme of the biblical text. The same problem can arise in storytelling. A storyteller may erroneously think that the story is the main thing, when the theme or lesson of the story must be the real focus.

A story is a vehicle that delivers a particular theme, plot, or point. When Jesus finishes the good Samaritan parable, it is as if he is rushing toward the completion of the story. He wants to get to the application. The only reason he has been telling this story is to cause his hearers to grapple with the profound question, "Which of these three do you think was a neighbor to the man who fell into the hands of robbers?" (10:36). Everything else is designed to facilitate the difficult yet obvious answer. The Samaritan is the real righteous one, even though Jesus' Jewish listeners believe that a Samaritan can never truly be a righteous man. That conundrum is the fulcrum upon which the story rests. The power is not in the story itself but in the meaning of the story. As in three-point sermons, the real power of the story is not in the story itself but in the application of the story to the lives of the hearers.

With Jesus as the model, Walsh gets this exactly right. His fifth point is crucial. A story that is effective must have a point, but it dare not have too many points. If you establish the *one* central theme of the passage, you can go a long way toward telling an unforgettable story. One. Not many, mind you, just one. That is the very heart of the KISS method.

In a narrative sermon on 1 Kings 17–18, I told the story from the perspective of the prophet Elijah. I began the sermon-story with the statement, "I know that God is faithful!" Then I detailed the ways in which God had been faithful to me (the character Elijah). I told how he fed me by the brook in the Kerith Ravine, east of the Jordan. I told about the miraculous oil and meal jars that never ran dry at the widow's home at Zarephath of Sidon. In each case, I returned to the main theme of knowing that God is faithful. The dramatic twist of the story occurs when Elijah confronts the unfaithful people of Israel with the words, "How long will you waver between two opinions?" (18:21). Elijah's real question was, "How long will you fail to realize the truth that, even in two years of drought, God has been faithful?" This is the central theme of the story. So I let the main point be the main point.

How to Make a Good Vegetable Stew

My wife makes a killer homemade vegetable stew. The best thing about it for me is that she puts in lots of meat. Have you ever gone to a restaurant and gotten the vegetarian version of vegetable stew? All carrots and tomatoes and no meat! The main point in a story is like the meat in the vegetable stew. At the same time, I notice that in making a good stew, my wife also adds a teaspoon of salt and pepper. Without the spices, the stew tastes bland. Arriving at a main theme or central point of a story does not mean that you should cut the story short or make it bland by omitting all the details. It simply means that you should get to the main point. While Jesus used parables as short, pithy teaching stories, narrative preaching can give you the opportunity to flesh out stories in more vivid terms.

Long ago, I learned that the secret to telling good sermon illustrations was having enough details. One can give new life to even familiar stories by adding greater detail to them. If the devil is in the details, then so, surely, is the Spirit of God in the details. Listeners are keen to learn more details of a biblical story. To the listener, details of a story are like the salt and pepper added to a stew: they enhance the flavor of the meal. If you think back to your early days of Bible study, you will remember moments when you came across details of a narrative that helped to put the story into an understandable context for you. From that context, greater depth, insight, and knowledge came flooding into your study session. Has it been too long since you have experienced that kind of revelation? If it has, then you should begin narrative preaching. Why? Because the preparation for narrative preaching takes you back into the discovery process of finding more and more details. Details become the hinge point upon which a narrative journey turns.

For instance, in a conference some years ago at the National Preaching Clinic in Dayton, Ohio, Pastor David Cox gave us an example of the importance of narrative details in preaching. He was preparing a sermon on the feeding of the five thousand. He became curious about the part of the text where the disciples took up twelve basketfuls of leftovers. "What do you do with leftovers?" he asked. That became the focus of his sermon. However, he discovered a detail that changed the way he thought about the story. He discovered that the text's word for *baskets* did not mean a large fruit-basket type of receptacle. Instead, this basket was more akin to a pouch that one might hang from a belt, to carry one's own lunch. In other words, the twelve baskets of leftovers were enough to feed each of the disciples their own lunch. After serving the five thousand, there was enough left over to feed the servers. How like God! If you serve him with everything you have, he will provide all your needs, even your sack lunch. Details, details, details.

Good storytelling lets you go through the details of a story with purpose. Intimate details in a biblical text can be used in a narrative sermon with greater effectiveness than in propositional preaching. When you find details on flora or fauna from the text, it enhances the scene in the mind's eye of the listener. If you run across an archaeological description of a house or structure, it helps to recreate that setting in the listener's brain. When you provide details, you provide opportunities for the hearer to begin thinking in close-ups rather than thinking in long-range shots. When I purchased my first camera and had the pictures developed, I realized that long-range shots left out the detail that a close-up gives. I found that close-ups were far more enjoyable pictures than faraway views of some landscape. Eventually, I learned to take shots of things far away by putting someone or something in the foreground. The object in the foreground gave something for the eye to engage while looking at the main subject in the distance. That is what detail does. It provides foreground, which brings the main point into focus in the background. It is the salt and pepper of the stew.

In the movie *Pleasantville* (1998), the two main characters are sucked into a television set showing a marathon of a 1950s TV family sitcom. They replace the son and daughter of the show's main family. As such, they enter into a world that is all black and white. The town is one-dimensional and cannot see beyond itself or the rather simplistic plots of the original TV shows. None of the townspeople change their routines. But as the two teenagers begin to interact with the people of the town, they introduce new concepts and ideas into the people's thinking. Finally, one of the townies drives down a street and sees a rose by the side of the road. But instead of being black and white, it is a bright red rose.

Imagine the chaos and questions of people who are suddenly thrust into a world full of color. It revolutionizes the town and the people in it. It creates panic, joy, tension, conflict, ecstasy, and a whole host of emotions and ideas that have never existed in this sleepy little village stuck in a bygone era. Why? Because when we see things in color, we see them in greater detail. And the greater the detail, the more interesting life becomes. It is not too much to say that the power of a story is in its details—and you as preacher get to add that color.

However, please recognize that you cannot make a good vegetable stew by dumping in a whole bottle of salt and a whole can of pepper. If you do, the spice overwhelms the flavor of the whole pot. You can add a dash of salt and pepper, a little here and a little there. To put it another way, a storyteller should eliminate needless details.[2] If you supply so much detail to the story that you get lost in the telling, you have lost your audience too.

Have you ever heard someone start to tell a story and forget whether the incident happened on Monday or a Tuesday? They spend so much time trying to get the day right that you quickly lose interest in the story they are trying to tell. Don't spend time in travelogue or bewildering background material that does not advance the story or help to clarify your main point.

HOW AND WHEN TO ADD VEGETABLES TO THE STEW

Have you ever wondered why you add vegetables to vegetable stew (beside the fact that the name of the dish is "vegetable" stew)? At least one of the reasons is that the texture

---

2. For more on this idea, see Walsh, *Art of Storytelling*, 68–70.

and taste of the vegetables adds variety to the dish, much like the salt and pepper do. Vegetables bring a contrasting texture and flavor to the meat and broth. When you eat a dish with multiple items in the main course, you do so because you like the flavor and texture, which allow your mouth to compare and contrast the different food items on your plate.

Like vegetables in the stew, details give you a greater opportunity to compare and contrast your story with other stories. The more details you know about the story, the more you can place the story in opposition to other familiar stories or strengthen the impact of your story by comparing it favorably with a different narrative that is better known. Recently, I told the story of Moses standing before the people of Israel in Exodus 18. He is standing before them as their judge, making decisions concerning their disputes and sharing his sense of the will of God for their lives. In reviewing the text, I happened upon the idea of comparing the upbringing of Moses with the upbringing of the nation he is now leading in the desert. Can they be any more different? Moses is a man of privilege, who grew up in pharaoh's household with the finest education of anyone in the world. His surroundings were palatial, and he wore the finest of fabrics, tailored to his dimensions and physique. His life was filled with satin and lace. He ate the finest foods from the farms of Egypt, brought by those who paid tribute to Pharaoh. His social surroundings were highly refined with music, exercise, culture, social graces, languages, art, and drama. He was trained to be a pharaoh and a leader of millions. He lived as a member of the royal class, a life of extreme privilege. Moses was used to having servants, not being one. His only understanding of slavery was watching others experience it. No one told Moses what to do. He spoke and others did his bidding.

Could the nation Moses now leads be any more different in background and upbringing? They were raised poor, uneducated, and repressed. The people of Israel were largely illiterate, uncultured, and unrefined. The Egyptians put them to forced labor or even slavery, and they were second- or third-class people in the Egyptian empire. They had known the lash, the whip, and the point of a spear. They had dirty hands from working in the fields, making bricks, building store cities and fortifications, or helping in rich Egyptians' homes. They had no rights, privileges, or standing in the community. Taskmasters told them what to do and when to do it from the moment they awoke in the morning till the time they retired at night. They never had their own police force or military. They had no judges or body of law. They had few, if any, public religious ceremonies or houses of worship. They lived a life of utter despair and poverty. They were *un*-royalty.

One might think that Moses got a cruel dose of reality when, after killing an Egyptian, he was forced to flee his royal lifestyle. The details prove otherwise. Moses, the fleeing fugitive, attached himself to the household of Jethro, eventually marrying his daughter. Who is Jethro? A rich rancher. We can appropriately call him a plantation owner, in that he owns flocks and grazing areas for his sheep. He is one of the richest men in that area of the world. So when Moses arrives back in Egypt after his encounter with God in the burning bush, he comes to be the leader of a people he does not know. He tells them that God has spoken with him, a God who has been silent for generations. Moses says God has called him to represent a people with whom he (Moses) has had no contact for forty years. How did such a man become a respected leader, so much so that they seek him out, from morning till night, to arbitrate their conflicts and help them understand the will of God for their lives?[3]

Put into a narrative form, contrasting Moses's upbringing with the hard life and times of the Israelite people, forms a compelling story that engages the reader. It is not just a story. After all, many people who hear such a story already know a great many of the details themselves. However, by repackaging the story in a compare-and-contrast mode, you bring freshness to the details and brightness to the story—whether it is old or new to the hearer. You have added some vegetables.

WHAT DOES VEGETABLE STEW TASTE LIKE?

All the details about making vegetable stew will interest no one but a few cooks. To those who aren't involved in cooking, a recipe is not all that engaging. But everyone is interested in what food tastes like. So how would you describe the taste of a really good vegetable stew? Can you describe your reaction upon eating an exceptionally good meal? Using some detail, describe the finest meal you have ever eaten. (Details of its appearance are fine, but it is far more compelling to describe the feelings, moods, emotions, and experiences of such an event.) My wife's vegetable stew was just another soup until I tasted it. Since then, it has become a holiday favorite and a family tradition. Walsh says it this way:

> The goal of a story is to stimulate the listeners' five senses, to draw them into the story. There should be enough description so the audience will see, hear, taste,

---

3. The details of this story can be found in Exodus 1–18.

smell, and feel everything going on. The old storytelling principle says, "Never state a fact if you can bring that fact to life." This is the difference between giving the essence of an event and being a storyteller.[4]

When I think of a story that has happened to me, I relive the event. Not only do I see the event, but I also feel the event. I experience the sensual aspects of the moment I am describing. I know how my wife's stew tastes and smells. I know what others say when they taste it and how they describe the experience. If I am trying to communicate a story, I must help the listener see not only what takes place but also become a player in the story. One teenager wrote, "I love the feeling of being inside the story."[5] That is the highest compliment you can pay a storyteller or someone who preaches narratively. It means that the listener has not just listened to you but also entered your story. It also means that the storyteller has not just given details but has recreated what is happening in the story. Walt Disney once received a letter from a man who said that he could use his voice to perfectly mimic a potato. While the rest of Walt's staff got a hearty laugh from the letter, Walt told his secretary to call the man up and offer him a job. The rest of his staff was dumbfounded by this. "But Walt," they said, "no one knows what a potato sounds like." Disney's reply? "Neither do I, but anyone who thinks they do needs to be working for the Walt Disney Company."

That's what happens when you move from fact-based details to life-based descriptions. You put emotions, feelings,

---

4. Walsh, *Art of Storytelling*, 71.
5. Ibid.

memories, attitudes, laughter, tears, pain, creativity, and pleasure into the telling of the story. Stories are not static things merely to be recounted. Narrative preaching is not making sure you tell every last detail associated with the text. Narrative preaching is telling a story in a way that enables the listener to enter and become a part of the story—emotionally, spiritually, and intellectually.

If you are a father, as I am, try telling the story of the birth of your children without mentioning the emotions, feelings, and wonder of the event. Try telling about the first time you told someone you loved them, but do it without experiencing the joy or pain of that moment. Try telling someone how you came to know Jesus Christ as your Savior without expressing the emotion of the new birth or the feeling of being forgiven. You simply cannot. Such stories are full of life. They are the signposts and altars of stone upon which the remembrances of life are placed. They are the stuff of life. If you tell your personal stories with vividness and emotion, then you should be able to tell the greatest story ever told with all the emotion and insight it deserves. "Description is not factual information. It is feelings and emotions that help the listener enter the world of the story. It is taking an ordinary action statement and expanding it. Description transforms statements of fact into exciting life experiences."[6]

VEGETABLE STEW IS BEST REHEATED

My wife firmly believes that her vegetable stew is even better after it has been prepared, refrigerated, and then served a second time. The flavors seem to seep into the broth even more after the dish becomes a leftover. Who am I to argue?

---

6. Ibid.

In the same way, remember that a good story or narrative sermon rarely comes out the way it should the first time you tell it. So good storytelling requires multiple tellings. The more you recite the story aloud, the more details you recall and the more comments you begin to make concerning the scene. When you reheat a narrative, you put more descriptive elements in the picture. You notice the interaction of characters and events more closely. As you narrate the story out loud, things pop into your mind that didn't come into your thought process the first time (or second time) you told it. These insights flesh out the story in greater and more compelling detail. If you have spent any time preaching, you already know this but may not fully realize how well you know it and how often you have proved it. Let me give you a few examples of how it is true.

Every preacher is faced with the daunting task of preparing new sermons each year for Advent and Easter. You go back year after year to many of the same texts and stories you have used many times before. However, when you tell the story of Jesus dying on the cross, don't you tell it with greater detail today than when you first started preaching? As you describe the sacrifice of Christ on the cross, don't you tell it with deeper feeling and more vivid description than you did years ago? Doesn't the empty tomb elicit more emotion now than it did when you first told the story? In your experience, hasn't the story of the virgin birth become even more joyful and celebrative in your mind each time you tell it? You don't approach these life-changing moments as mere recitations of fact, do you? If these all-too-familiar New Testament images have become more intense and more powerful as the years go by, then surely a narrative story will become more drenched with descriptive elements the more you tell it. When you reheat the narrative, two things happen:

1. The details of narrative come into sharper focus in your mind and become more distinct, like putting a camera into focus.

2. The descriptions of the interaction of characters and events become more intense in your mind and more real in your telling.

Try it out. I think you will come to believe the wise counsel of my wife: vegetable stew (and stories) are better when they are served again.

CONCLUSION

It is a powerful thing to enter into a story. It is an even more amazing thing to lead others into a story. Good storytellers and good narrative sermons accomplish just that.

Gloria Gaither is one of the world's great storytellers. She has written best-selling books and inspired thousands of people in concerts around the world, simply by sharing her stories. One of her song-stories is titled "I Walked Today Where Jesus Walks." This poignant song has a marvelous story behind it. Gloria audited a class at her alma mater, Anderson University, in which one of the requirements was to go on a class trip to Chicago, where they visited and served in some of the poorest neighborhoods of the city. Instead of writing a term paper or thesis about her class project, she wrote the words to this song. It recorded her reaction to the experience of spending time with people in abject poverty. As you read the story in Gloria's song, you enter the story. You see the children and homeless souls in need, men who have lost hope, cars going by without stopping or even noticing the plight of the hungry and needy. More important, you will find yourself placing

Jesus in the midst of these dire circumstances. When you see him walking down the streets of Chicago ministering to the down and out, then you too have entered the story.

> I walked today where Jesus walks, down the crowded
> streets,
> Where the children have no place to play,
> Where the homeless wait for life to take them in
> Yes, I walked with Jesus there today.
>
> I saw the Lord behind the eyes of the broken men;
> And I felt His wounded hand reach out.
> And as the careless traffic sped along the other side,
> I saw Jesus walk the streets today.
>
> Where the least of all find no place to turn,
> And they fall without a name—
> Jesus walks with these, the hungry and the lost,
> Offering water from a cup and bread;
>
> The Bread of Life, the Living stream where teeming
> millions cross
> To find that God, yes, God Himself walks there.
> Where the least of all find no place, they turn
> To find that God, yes, God himself—
> God, yes, God Himself walks there,
> He walks there.

Enter the story and bring others with you. When you do, you will find that God himself walks there. This is the power of narrative preaching. Come enter the world of sacred story.

7

PREACHING NARRATIVE SERMONS IN UNUSUAL PLACES
MOVING NARRATIVE INTO THE MAINSTREAM

And when in scenes of glory I sing the new, new song,
'Twill be the old, old story that I have loved so long.

BREAKING DOWN WALLS AND BRIDGING GAPS

Someone once asked me how often I do narrative sermons. My answer was simply, "All the time." What they really wanted to know was how often I did first-person narratives in the pulpit. I do them periodically but not weekly. My goal in writing this book is not to influence preachers to begin doing first-person narrative sermons every week. That will not happen, and I doubt that it should. As my son Jonathan, the seminarian, said to me when I began writing this book, "Dad, I like propositional truth sermons." Well, so do I, and I often preach them. However, narrative preaching is also a tool that every preacher should have at his or her disposal.

I recently attended a conference in Sacramento where Becky Pippert, the author of *Out of the Saltshaker and into the World* (1979), was speaking. She said, "We know that postmoderns learn truth better in narrative than in any other form." If that is true, then we have to break down the barriers that prevent us from preaching more narratively if we are to reach the generations to come.

There must be a commitment to story as part of our basic theology. To do this places us at the very heart of sound theological method, not opposed to it. Gerhard Laughlin puts it this way:

> Long before it was fashionable to be non-foundational, Hans Frei (1922–1988) had learnt from Karl Barth (1886–1968) that Christian faith rests not upon universal reason or human self-consciousness, but is sustained through and as a commitment to a story. The story is not supported by anything else, by another story, theory or argument. The story is simply told, and faith is a certain way of telling it, a way of living and embodying it; a habit of the heart.[1]

In other words, to reach the current generation and engage the generations already in the church, we must appeal to and tell out the story on which we base the entirety of our faith. All narrative preaching embraces this theological truth.

MOVING INTO THE MAINSTREAM

When I was a pastor in Florida, our congregation had a number of retired pastors. One of them, Lowell Hunt, had served as a pastor for many years. He had a wealth of experience to share, for which I was grateful. One Lenten season, as we were preparing for a Maundy Thursday service (including foot washing), I lamented the fact such a small portion of the congregation would participate. Lowell wondered if

---

1. Laughlin, *Telling God's Story*, 33.

it wasn't because of the outmoded manner of the service. "We no longer live in a culture that washes feet as a normal practice of social graces," he observed. "It is out of the mainstream of our cultural setting." He then told me about a foot-washing service he had attended many years earlier at a conference with the great Quaker theologian D. Elton Trueblood. Near the end of the conference, Dr. Trueblood told the group that they were going to have one last activity that would help them understand the role of service and humility in ministry. He talked about the foot-washing experience of Jesus and the disciples in John 13. Then he told the ministers that they were going to put this into a modern context. Immediately, several members of the hosting organization came out to the ministers, seated in a circle. In the middle of the circle, they placed boxes of brushes, shoe polish, and cloth. Dr. Trueblood then asked them to shine each other's shoes. Lowell said he had never understood the meaning of foot washing until he shined another man's shoes. Dr. Trueblood took an ancient ritual and put it in a modern setting. He applied it in a new and meaningful way.

For narrative preaching to have an impact on our culture, we must begin to see the application of narrative as more than just periodic adventures into novel ways of telling a story. Narrative preaching must become part of the mainstream of everyday Christian life.

First, we can make narrative sermons part of the mainstream of our preaching schedule. It lends itself quite well to ministers who do series preaching. If you are planning a series of four or five sermons on a biblical character (such as Elijah), you can do all of those sermons in a narrative style. Here is a possible series using Elijah as the subject:

PREACHING THE STORY

1. "Confronting the King" (1 Kings 17:1; 18:16–20, 41–46). This could be a first-person narrative sermon retelling the confrontations between Ahab and Elijah. You could narrate this story as either Elijah or Ahab. The sermon could have as its theme the idea of standing up for truth against intimidating foes, speaking truth to power, confronting evil by the power of God, or submitting to the Lord.

2. "The Faithfulness of God" (1 Kings 17). Using the character of Elijah, retrace ways in which God was faithful to you during this time of drought. You can story the scenes of the birds and Kerith Ravine, the widow of Zarephath, and the return to Mount Carmel. The final scene can be Elijah returning to the mount and confronting the people with the challenge of 18:21. The theme of God's faithfulness from the experiences of Elijah during the drought will prepare your hearers for the confrontation with the unfaithful people of Elijah's day, challenging them not to waver any longer. It can be a powerful story that challenges your own congregation to stand up for God because he has been faithful to them in so many ways.

3. "Trusting the Lord in Dire Circumstances" (1 Kings 17–18). This could be a third-person narrative in which you become an implied character in the biblical story. Become a farmer during the drought in Israel. Have Elijah stop by your home for a drink of water on his way to see Ahab and for another drink on his way out of town. You can describe the drought and your struggle between believing in God or turning to Baal, the god of fertility and harvest. The implied character can help you to

describe the struggle that most of us have as we seek to be true to God, even when the situation is not encouraging. Another way of approaching the same theme would be to become Obadiah. He appears in 18:1–16 and could be the source for the same kind of emphasis.

4. "Victory in the Lord" (1 Kings 18:16–46). Here is the dramatic confrontation between Elijah and the prophets of Baal. It may be best to describe this part of the story through the eyes of a narrator who is able to observe the whole scene. The story is so powerful that you can tell it in great detail without losing the audience. Its issues or themes are striking, and you can develop them as you see fit. Certainly, the theme of the Lord's victory over evil is one theme. There are others you may prefer to explore as you go along.

This is merely one example of a series you might preach using narrative sermons. Certainly, you can also infuse new life into a more traditional sermon series that one bases on propositional-truth passages. The point is that narrative sermons can fit into any preaching schedule or process. You can communicate the theme of a sermon series through narrative as well as other methods of sermon preparation and delivery.

CHANGING THE PERCENTAGES

Second, you can bring narrative preaching into the mainstream of everyday life by breaking into the narrative to make a current application of a biblical truth. You can accomplish this best by using a narrator approach to the text.[2] If you are narrating a story, it is quite acceptable to drop out of narrative on occasion and comment on its application. Actually, it is quite effective. Once you have made your point, go back to the story and continue from where you left off. Recently I preached a sermon on the story of David, Nabal, and Abigail based on 1 Samuel 25. To make sure everyone understood the confrontation, I went back into previous chapters of 1 Samuel and recounted the tension between King Saul and David. (Every time I introduced a new character into the story, I brought up someone from the congregation and gave them a sign to hold with the name of that character. My helpers had no lines to speak, but their placards helped the congregation follow the story.) As the story unfolded, I occasionally stopped the narrative to make an application concerning each person and their situation.

For instance, this was part of a sermon series on family issues, so I used the interference of Saul in the marriage of David and Michal to make some comments about being a responsible in-law, staying out of the marriage dynamics of your children. In the same way, I broke from the narrative to comment on the time Michal protected her husband from her father's henchmen, who had been sent to kill him (1 Sam 19:9–17). I reminded the congregation that when you get married, you leave your father and mother and join your spouse. If you ever have to choose between your parents and your spouse, you have already done that at the marriage altar. You chose your spouse and left your home to make a new home. After making that point, I returned to the narrative.

This may be the most effective way to bridge the gap between propositional preaching and narrative preaching. Reverse the proportions. In propositional preaching, the points of application comprise about 75 percent of the sermon and narrative comprises the remaining 25 percent. Narrative

---

2. See chap. 3, "Step 1: Moving into the Text; The Narrator Approach."

preaching reverses the figures: you devote 75 percent of your time and effort to telling the story in some detail. The points of application take up only 25 percent of the sermon. Why so little time for application? Because the story makes the application for you. The Bible becomes even more dominant in your preaching; it becomes the substance behind every point you make. Instead of stating your opinion, you are making application of a story God has given his people.

If Becky Pippert is right, we are moving into a time when story-based sermons will have a greater impact. You can be part of that movement by switching the emphasis in your sermons. You will find that your messages are not less relevant but more so. Sometimes we church leaders struggle with whether to be relevant at the expense of being biblical. Narrative sermons do not pose such a dilemma. By preaching narrative sermons, we can be both culturally relevant and biblically reliant.

VARIATIONS ON A PREACHING THEME

Most preachers have the spiritual gift of continuation. When given opportunity to speak, they are more than willing to do so. However, if they have less than the traditional twenty-five-minute sermon slot, they find it difficult to comply. You may be like this. However, another type of narrative preaching can be quite effective for those who have the personal discipline to give a sermon in a shorter time period! Not all narrative stories are best presented in the main preaching time. There are various ways in which a narrative story can contribute to the worship service without using the preaching time. In such cases, they should be shorter rather than longer stories. If you can fit a story into a ten-minute time frame, you have a wealth of possibilities. Let me cite some examples.

My wife and I have teamed up to teach the stories behind some of the great hymns of the church. It is a great musical partnership: Joanie is a wonderful pianist and singer, and I can tell stories. Numerous information sources on the Internet can help you learn how lyricists came to write hymns, worship songs, or choruses. In some cases, the stories of choral music may also be available. These stories can enhance the experience of worship. If you apply the principles taught in these pages and use them in this manner, you can add a wonderful worship element to the service.[3]

Many choir musicals now give the option of including a testimony or personal sharing during the presentation. Even if they do not, some musicals could be easily adapted to include a story time. If the musical centers on a particular theme or a main character, a first-person account or faith story could enhance the music. In such a case, be sure that the story is of proper length to fit the overall presentation. If you manage your time well and produce something that enhances the musical's impact, there is a natural match between a choral presentation and an effective narrative.

In many churches, children's sermons are an effective part of the worship service. I have seen leaders present them at center stage during the service or in a separate gathering for children outside the sanctuary during the worship time. Either way, children love to hear stories. My sons loved to have us read them a story as they were growing up. Telling a biblical story to children in front of adults gives you an

---

3. Amazon.com lists several books on hymn stories, including Kenneth W. Osbeck, *101 Hymn Stories*; idem, *101 More Hymn Stories*; Robert J. Morgan, *Then Sings My Soul: 150 of the World's Greatest Hymn Stories*; Jane Stuart Smith, *Great Christian Hymn Writers*. A Google search or look in a Christian bookstore will provide you with more stories than you can possibly use.

opportunity to speak directly to children while also speaking to the adults. Time constraints will cause you to tighten up the story process during the worship hour, but you will find rich material to share with young children, and they will readily respond to the story with their faces, hearts, and minds. At the last minute, one church asked me to lead a chapel service for the elementary kids. Without much time to prepare a story, I took out a storybook designed to teach children the concept of following God's will and being holy in our actions.[4] The book did all this in the context of a story about a dragon, knights on a quest, and a small boy who was an apprentice. It was a fairly long story to read (about fifteen minutes), but the kids loved it and were in rapt attention.

Many churches hold retreats for leaders or other groups within the church. In informal settings such as camps or retreat centers, the story format is a welcome change from the routine lecture or propositional message. When I was in college, one summer I traveled with two other students representing the college on something called "Camp Tour." It was a life-changing experience for me to travel from youth camp to youth camp during those nine weeks. As we learned our roles and responsibilities, we found that our most effective ministry was during the evening campfire times. That setting gave us opportunity to involve the youth in a new kind of experience. We would sing the lively camp songs that everyone uses, and eventually a guy on the team would lead a time of testimony. Finally, I would tell a story of some dramatic event or idea that we had picked up during our travels together. The youth responded tremendously to the campfire services. We

---

4. I read Bishop, *Squire and the Scroll*. Bishop, *Princess and the Kiss*, is also an excellent story to read or tell to youth or children.

often had greater spiritual impact during the campfire times than we did in the services at the campground tabernacles. Being out under the stars in a pair of jeans and sneakers can make a formal sermon unwieldy. On the other hand, stories fit that occasion amazingly well. In the rustic setting of camps and retreats, try being more narrative and less formal.

NARRATING FINAL THINGS

I once received a wonderful note from one of my parishioners following a narrative sermon. In part she wrote, "Thank you for doing what you do so well,...collecting stories of everyday life and applying God's Word." This note came to me following the funeral of her mother, and she was describing the sermon I shared at the funeral. Funerals are an integral part of what we do in pastoral ministry. In spite of that, seminaries rarely teach us how to prepare and deliver a funeral sermon. Others generally tell us, "Remember that you are preaching to the living, not the dead." That's a valid perspective, but it does not give helpful guidance on exactly how we should put a funeral sermon together.

Funeral services generally fall into one of three categories. First is the liturgical style, offering all the elements already put together and simply changing the name of the deceased to fit the current funeral. It is a cookie-cutter approach to preaching that concentrates on telling mourners the great truths about eternal life and reminding them of the hope God gives us in the Scriptures.

Second is the funeral service that requires participation by family members or friends. During the service, someone comes forward to tell the congregation about all the things that made the deceased so special. Usually, this speaker mostly gives general comments about the person's character, perhaps with some details that the family wants to make sure everyone knows and understands. We usually call this presentation the eulogy, and it often stands apart from the pastor's funeral sermon. Some funerals even do this impromptu, providing or passing a microphone and inviting members of the congregation to share their remembrances of the deceased.

Third is the service where the pastor delivers both the eulogy and the funeral sermon himself. In one pastorate, I assisted in my first funeral service three days after arriving as senior pastor. The family asked the previous pastor to conduct the funeral since I had only met the deceased on his deathbed. The retired pastor spoke twice, sharing a eulogy first and later delivering a funeral sermon. I could not distinguish between the two. Both seemed to be funeral messages.

When I first entered pastoral ministry in Hickory, North Carolina, my mentor was a great preacher named Forrest Plants. Forrest had a distinguished long-term pastorate in that church. He was an author, accomplished preacher, national leader, and a fascinating man to work with. Forrest had many gifts and talents, but it wasn't until I began assisting him at funerals that I discovered his real gift. He was the finest funeral preacher I have ever heard. For two years, I heard him preach dozens of funeral messages. He did numerous services for the parishioners he had served for many years. Because he was so good at it, funeral homes in the area also called him to conduct funerals for families who had no church home. During those two years, he held as many funerals for people outside the church as he did for those inside the church. The quality of what he shared and the style that he used never varied. He was always scriptural, always comforting, always helpful, and always narrative. How do you preach a narrative funeral sermon for someone you have never met or hardly know? Forrest taught me his secret, and I gladly share it with you (with his permission and blessing). I have used this secret for more than thirty years, and it works wonders.

Forrest always sat down with the grieving family and asked them to tell him about their loved one. Whether he knew them well or not at all, he started the same way: "Tell me about your loved one." The information and stories they shared were healing to the family. They would sit around and laugh and cry at the memories of the one they loved. Forrest took notes. He jotted down the stories. He would then determine which scriptural passage fit best (almost always a narrative section), and he would then put the deceased person in the story—either literally or figuratively.

I remember one funeral that Forrest preached for an elderly lady from the congregation. She had been a quiet and unassuming woman who spent her time in the background serving others, instead of being in the foreground taking credit or receiving honors. She was the epitome of a humble servant. Forrest read Matthew 5:5, "Blessed are the meek, for they will inherit the earth." He began by telling the story of the Sermon on the Mount. He described Jesus and the surroundings. He spoke of the crowd and the setting on the mountainside. As he was weaving the story, he imaginatively took the audience out of the sanctuary for a moment or two.

Then, suddenly, Forrest introduced a new element into the story: "Jesus looked at the back of the crowd as he spoke and he said, 'Blessed are the poor in spirit, for theirs is the kingdom of heaven'—and he stopped. Then Jesus pointed his finger and said, 'Minnie, why don't you come on up closer? Come on up, come on up here with me.'" With that, Forrest introduced the deceased into the biblical scene. As he continued to share the story of the Beatitudes and the setting of the

Sermon on the Mount, he kept inviting Minnie (not her real name) to "come on up, come up here with me." By the time he had finished the story, Minnie had come from the back of the crowd to stand beside Jesus. In the final scene, Jesus took her hand and said, "Come on, Minnie. Come on up with me." Saying that, Jesus led her into the heavenly realms.

That was almost three decades ago, and I can still remember the moment—and the sermon. If you want to make your funeral messages meaningful and your ministry to grieving families broader, then make your funeral sermons narrative.

You can also make funeral sermons narrative by simply taking the information you have gained about the deceased and using it to highlight the points you have in the sermon. This often alleviates the problem of "preaching someone into heaven." One of the most common problems that a preacher encounters in funeral messages is what to say if the person is not a believer or has lived a terribly sinful life. If you try to say nice things about someone like that, you will have some rather awkward moments in the funeral. This is equally true for marginal believers, about whose relationship with the Lord you know little. How far can you go in asserting their faith if they didn't go far to assert it while they were alive? In both cases, you can preach from the life of the person without leaving the scriptural truths behind.

For example, I have often recognized the hardships of someone who has died and highlighted that human hardship, suffering, and pain prepare us for death. I remind those assembled that we must all prepare for the inevitable end of life. I point out that the deceased had time to prepare. I ask, "What are you doing with your time to prepare for what must and will take place?" By using the life and experience of the deceased as a general illustration, I make the sermon far more personal than the family expects and far more biblically relevant than just using the text without connecting it to that person's life.

In the course of more than thirty years of pastoral ministry, I do not believe I have ever delivered a funeral sermon that was not narrative in nature. In funeral sermons, we have such an incredible opportunity to connect with people who are normally unwilling to sit through a sermon or even attend a church service. If we do not take advantage of the opportunity to share the good news at this point, we are missing a God-given moment. But if we try to explain theology at a funeral service to bridge the communication gap between the believing and skeptical communities, we are fooling ourselves. *Narrative* bridges the gap. It gives us a methodology to bring comfort to the bereaved and the gospel message to the congregation in a way that they can hear and understand.

STORIES REACH OUT AS WELL AS IN

One of the most instructive biblical stories about the effective use of narrative is the story of Philip and the Ethiopian eunuch.

> Then Philip ran up to the chariot and heard the man reading Isaiah the prophet. "Do you understand what you are reading?" Philip asked.
>
> "How can I," he said, "unless someone explains it to me?" So he invited Philip to come up and sit with him.
>
> The eunuch was reading this passage of Scripture:
> "He was led like a sheep to the slaughter,
> and as a lamb before the shearer is silent,
> so he did not open his mouth.
> In his humiliation he was deprived of justice.
> Who can speak of his descendants?

For his life was taken from the earth."
The eunuch asked Philip, "Tell me, please, who is the
prophet talking about, himself or someone else?" Then
Philip began with that very passage of Scripture and
told him the good news about Jesus. (Acts 8:30–35)

The eunuch has just come from Jerusalem and likely a
meeting with the elders of Israel. He is seeking to understand
and embrace a belief in one God, using a story unfamiliar
to him and yet trying to learn. His problem is that he cannot understand the Isaiah text. He needs an explanation.
What do you think Philip should do? Should he give him a
propositional truth or a theological lecture, or should he tell
him a narrative-based story of the truth? Philip decides to
tell him the story of the Christ (the "good news"). Philip has
a narrative text in front of him (the story of Christ's passion
prophesied in Isaiah 53), and he uses it to tell the story of
Jesus and what happened to him on the cross, at the tomb,
and in the intervening months. The true story so moves the
eunuch that he embraces Christ with enthusiasm. He is not
content to wait any longer to witness to his faith. A pool of
water comes into view, and Philip baptizes the new believer.
This is evangelism at its purest and best.

Narrative stories can be incredibly effective as outreach
tools. One church planter started a new congregation with a
clown ministry in a local park. Imagine reaching out to the
community and planting a church in a clown suit, in a park!
While the clown presentations were integral to the church
planting, the minister's use of stories and narrative became a
vital part of the congregation's continuing outreach as well.

Most professional storytellers have a circuit of places
open to them. John Walsh lists some of those places in

bullet fashion: libraries, women's clubs, YMCA/YWCA, Boy Scouts, Girl Scouts, schools (especially Christian schools that have chapel services), 4-H clubs, service groups, and others.[5] In these settings you may be hesitant or unable to tell a biblical story. Do not panic! You can develop narrative stories around hymns (see above), historical events, great Christian statesmen, historical characters, or even biblical characters, told from a historical or political point of view rather than a faith-based point of view.

CONCLUSION

This is not an exhaustive listing of the ways in which you can use your narrative abilities. I mean to spark your imagination and help you realize that you can use narrative in more settings than you may at first think possible. I have not mentioned the narrative possibilities that exist for other kinds of children's sermons or VBS programs or other events where many local churches incorporate the use of biblical characters in some form of first-person narrative or question-and-answer session. Sunday school classes often invite an individual to come into the class and play the part or tell the story of some biblical character. These examples of narrative preaching have become quite common in the Christian education of the local church. However, to limit the use of narrative to these common settings would remove from your toolbox a vital component of your teaching and preaching ministry.

Let your imagination soar. Remember, Jesus was a storyteller. You can be one too!

---

5. Walsh, *Art of Storytelling*, 151. Walsh also has chapters on how to organize a storytelling event and how to use narratives in an educational setting. In addition, his appendices supply a wealth of material on how to develop stories and find storytelling resources.

8

BARRIERS IN PREACHING
MOVING IN FRONT OF THE PEOPLE

I love to tell the story! 'Twill be my theme in glory—
To tell the old, old story of Jesus and his love.

OUT FROM BEHIND THE SACRED DESK

One problem that has arisen in the course of church history is that the architectural norms of the sanctuary have made a separation between the preaching of the Word and the involvement of the people. The pulpit has become the sacred desk and is used by most preachers as a lectern, behind which they stand during the sermon. Over time, we have begun referring to the pulpit as a place and not just a mere piece of furniture. Protestant churches have dubbed the pulpit as a sacred place because it is where preachers speak the Word of God. The church expects those who stand behind the pulpit to share, not their own words, but the Word of God as the Scriptures reveal it. The pulpit becomes the center for preaching the Word. Therefore, in common understanding, anyone who enters the pulpit indeed stands behind a so-called sacred desk because they stand in the spot where the Holy Spirit speaks.

Many denominational manuals caution ministers against using the pulpit for anything less than preaching God's truth. For instance, the Seventh-Day Adventists' *Church Manual* cautions: "In view of these considerations, it must be evident that the church cannot confer upon any individual the right to exploit personal views and opinions from the pulpit. The sacred desk must be reserved for the preaching of the sacred truths of the Divine Word and the presentation of denominational plans and policies for the advancement of the work of God."[1] Such cautions are well-founded, and those who preach from the pulpit should heed them.

However, this tradition has also made the pulpit a barrier between the preaching of the Word and God's people. We have incorporated so much church furniture into the platform/chancel area that a person needs real dexterity to find the way up to the platform. Church architects think there should be a physical separation between the holy place where preachers share the Word of God and the common area where the congregation stands. Elevation of the platform has added to the idea that there is a separation. Early in my ministry, I was in a church sanctuary where I watched the preacher ascend a long flight of stairs to the pulpit, about ten feet above the platform. I have been in other church buildings where the pulpit is ornate and one must step up to the pulpit. By adding a communion table, altars, or kneeling benches, modesty rails or panels, and plants for color, we have created a definite barrier between what happens on the platform and what is happening in the pew.

In the same way, robes and vestments separate clergy and laity. The church intends the minister's special garments

---

1. Seventh-Day Adventists, *Church Manual*, 207.

to differentiate the offices of pastor and laity, much like the robe of a judge differentiates the judge from lawyers and others in the courtroom. The judge's robe represents the fact that the person sitting behind the bench is not the authority; instead, the law is; Likewise, the priest's robes say that it is not the person but the office that is authoritative, not the priest but the Word of God. While all of this symbolism can create powerful visual meanings, the practical effect is to further separate God's Word from the people who are supposed to hear the Word. A simple review of the Gospels shows you that Jesus used little if any formalized structures to preach the good news. He stood behind no pulpit, rarely went into synagogues or the temple to minister or teach, and donned no sacred garments. Instead, he spoke in open fields, private homes, and from lakes or mountainsides. In everything that he did, he disdained anything that separated him from the crowd or God from the ordinary person. I have the feeling that Jesus might not take as high a view of our architectural norms as we do!

When I was first ordained into ministry in the Church of God, my mother and father were present for the ordination service. They were proud of their son, so they gave me two gifts following the service. My mother was an Episcopalian, so her church experience revolved around the traditions and practices of the Episcopal Church. She found it difficult to accept the less formal ways in which the Church of God expresses the truths of God. As a result, she gave me a clerical collar and a minister's alb. However, for someone in a less formal church group, these gifts were not generally practical. I did use the collar once to visit patients after a hospital refused entrance to me because I looked too young. Over the years, countless parishioners have used my alb to dress up as a shepherd in a Christmas play or some other kind of biblical character. Although my mother's gifts were not practical for the church setting in which I pastored, it was her way of expressing that since the church had duly recognized me, I should look the part. Everyone tends to view their own church's architecture and traditions as normative.

Try changing those traditions and see what happens. Have you ever moved a pulpit out of the sanctuary or off the platform in a church where you are pastor? I did once and ended up with more headaches than I care to recall. Someone had donated the pulpit in memory of a deceased family member; somehow they had vested the whole meaning of the worship service in that piece of wooden chancel furniture. Who was I to move what decades of tradition had placed there? No matter how unwieldy the piece or how crowded it makes the platform look, it must be used.

I have visited Colonial Williamsburg several times during my life and sat in the pews of Bruton Parish Church. Thomas Jefferson, George Washington, Richard Henry Lee, George Wythe, Patrick Henry, and George Mason once sat in those pews. The sanctuary has retained its eighteenth-century style and form. It is a moving experience to sit in that historic church. It still is a functioning Episcopal congregation, so I have enjoyed an evening vespers service and worshiped in a Sunday morning service. On one occasion when I was visiting the historic village on a Sunday, there was an announcement that the church would hold a different kind of service outside, beside one of the buildings in the town. I and others decided to attend. We gathered in a brush arbor and listened to a sermon delivered by a Methodist circuit-riding preacher! Dressed in eighteenth-century garb and using a sermon published in the 1770s, he preached as we stood under the trees. We needed no formal church architecture or furniture. I'm sure people needed none centuries ago when an actual preacher held a meeting in the same place.

One of the problems we have in the church today is that the authority of Scripture is taking a back seat to the traditions of the church or the expectations of the parishioners. Surely the Word has enough authority in and of itself that it does not require a wooden lectern to give it credence. Some would say that taking away the sacred desk can decrease the respect some have for you as a preacher and for the words the Holy Spirit gives through you. In spite of this, today's churches are moving away from platforms filled with furniture and the traditional pulpit. While it may push the envelope of acceptance in your church setting, consider removing the pulpit or at least moving away from the pulpit. Preaching is a form of communication. We should question anything that hinders the effective communication of the gospel or introduces barriers between the preaching of the Word and people hearing it.

With churches today challenging the meaning of the sanctuary's traditional setup, it is not hard to see that we need to find ways to dissolve the separation between the preaching of the Word of God and those who hear the Word. If you move out from behind the so-called sacred desk, you better prepare yourself for the experience of preaching narratively. The storytelling nature of their sharing forces those who preach first-person narrative sermons to move away from the pulpit and closer to the congregation. If you begin to move away from the pulpit while using your current style of preaching, you will find it infinitely easier to move away from it when you do narrative preaching.

BRIDGING THE COMMUNICATION GAP

Communication becomes far more effective when a public speaker moves from behind a lectern and stands closer to the crowd, with no barrier between them. A few years ago, Elizabeth Dole addressed the Republican National Convention. Instead of standing at the lectern and reading from Plexiglas prompters, which have become a staple of political speechmaking, she gave a stirring address without using a prompter or notes. After the speech, most of the news commentators said they were impressed by her style. Certainly, the most memorable speech that President George W. Bush has given was after the 9/11 tragedies, when he stood next to a firefighter in the rubble of the World Trade Centers. The president spoke without notes or lectern through a bullhorn to the crowd, the American people, and the world. Public speakers who dare to step out from behind the barriers between themselves and their listeners find that the communication quotient rises exponentially.

To apply this to our preaching, we must find ways to move out from behind the pulpit and stand face-to-face with our people. It can feel like a naked thing to stand in front of a congregation without hiding behind or leaning on something, but it is also tremendously freeing. Most experienced preachers do not read from manuscripts.[2] If you use an outline in some form, you are in the majority of preachers. If that is the case, how much of the outline do you read during a sermon? The typical answer is, Not much. Then why not abandon your notes, leave the pulpit, and stand in front of the congregation? You can always

---

2. There are notable exceptions to this. One of my mentors, Dr. Sam Hines, preached from a manuscript during his entire ministry and was one of the great pulpiteers of the twentieth century.

wander back to gather your notes or read from the Word. But if you preach while standing on your own and not relying on notes, you have obtained a powerful communication tool. When you preach without barriers, you create a dialogue with the hearers that you do not have while standing behind a piece of furniture. Even the way you process information and express ideas will change when you interact with an audience rather than deliver a speech from behind a desk.

A weakness of homiletics instruction today is that we do not prepare ministerial students to fully engage the congregation with their preaching. While hermeneutics and textual preparation are crucial and vital, the delivery of that information in an unobtrusive manner is also crucial. The preacher must create an atmosphere in which the hearer is able to fully understand the truth that the Holy Spirit has revealed. The delivery of a sermon is what hooks the hearer into listening for the revealed truth of God's Word.

Why is this whole discussion necessary? Because it is important for you to understand that you cannot do effective narrative preaching behind a pulpit. Storytelling is a campfire activity. It is something you do when a group gathers around you. It is not formal or stuffy. A story is a picture that begins to roll through the minds of hearers as it rolls off the tongue of the storyteller. Moving away from a pulpit takes you to a place where storytelling is possible—out in the open.

Storytellers look their audience in the eye and lean toward them a bit as they make their opening statement. They speak *with* people rather than *to* them. By its very nature, storytelling is a dialogical experience. In a classroom, we seek to have students engage in a dialogue.

When we teach the value of prayer, we stress the importance of listening for God's voice. When we teach new believers to read and study the Word, we implore them to listen for the Holy Spirit's counsel. In the same way, preaching must be a dialogue between preacher and hearer. While some preachers can still engage in a dialogue with their congregation while standing behind a pulpit, I am convinced that it is an impediment for many preachers and most congregations.

Storytellers dare to stand in front of a group, comforted only by the fact that their story is greater than the person telling the story. Storytellers strive to see their audience, because the dynamic of story is found in the reaction of the hearer to the power of the picture being drawn. Storytelling is interactive. While your hearers need not get up out of their seats to enter the story, you must get up out of your seat to invite them into the story. You should remove or eliminate anything that distracts them from entering the story or inhibits their movement to the setting of the story, so that they can interact with the truth.

CREATING CHARACTER FROM WITHIN

One year on an Easter break, I traveled with the drama department of my college. The play we staged in churches was entitled *Christ in the Concrete City*.[3] During the performance, the characters in the play alternate between being a speaking choir and being a variety of characters. I served as six different characters during the course of the drama. Normally, an actor depends on scene changes, costume

---

3. Turner, *Christ in the Concrete City*.

changes, or some other device to give the appearance of a different character. However, our director never allowed us to leave the stage. We never changed costumes. We never had any scenery. We had nothing to create another character except our voices or our mannerisms. It was an incredible challenge to create a new character without using props.

As preachers, we, on a weekly basis, face the daunting task of speaking to roughly the same group of folks. We do this month in and month out, year in and year out. How do you create a new character every week? How do you create variety in sermon delivery or sermonic practice? Most of our sermons have become almost liturgical in nature. They are too predictable from week to week. The sermon begins with an illustration, moves to three points, ends with a closing illustration, and finishes with an appeal for commitment. Most parishioners can tell you the form and style of their pastor's preaching from memory. Preachers much in demand have created powerful presentations that have dynamic diversity to them. Charles Swindoll, John Maxwell, Billy Graham, Bob Russell, and Tony Evans—all these great preachers take a time-tested sermonic style and infuse it with both the power and the creativity of personality to make an effective preaching experience.

But what of the rest of us? We who work hard at the preparation and delivery of sermons in thousands upon thousands of less celebrated pulpits—what can we do? How do we create interest and variety in our preaching experience? Even our modest-sized congregations deserve to have a powerful and creative ministry of preaching. How can we give them that?

CREATING VARIETY

One way to add variety to your preaching is to mix narrative-type sermons with the more propositional sermons you normally do. As we have seen, there are many kinds of narrative-based sermons; hence, the genre itself offers you many kinds of changes that you can add to the sermon schedule. Another option is to introduce costuming and scenery in your preaching. After attending a worship service at Willow Creek Community Church and finding that the teaching pastor spent most of the sermon sitting at a table with a plasma screen hanging in the background, I began to consider whether we needed to take a deeper look, not just at church furniture, but at the whole idea of how we preachers present ourselves to the congregation.

PROPS AND SCENERY

While the church rarely uses either of these words, it spends a lot of time and money on the ecclesiastical version of props and scenery. We spend considerable time and effort on sanctuary colors, banners, plants, chairs, screens, projection images, and candles. All of these belong under the broad category of scenery or props. Scenery is whatever you present to make the eyes of the congregation focus on the matter at hand. You may have a waterfall in the background or a PowerPoint image on the screen. You may have a banner or a sign about this week's theme. You may have a backdrop of colorful plants or greenery. We design each of these to provide an appropriate atmosphere in which to worship. How far should we take this? Should we rearrange the platform furniture? Should we position anything that is visually noticeable so that it serves as a backdrop for the preaching of the Word?

Sometimes even simple props can enhance the worship experience. I preached the funeral service of a man in our congregation who had been an outstanding volunteer. He had spent countless hours painting, cleaning out gutters, rewiring electrical needs, and providing a host of other maintenance services for the church and several Christian missionary organizations. At his funeral I placed a stepladder on the platform and put several items on it that illustrated Roger's life. It was a simple but effective prop. One question you should ask as you prepare for preaching is, What decoration would enhance the subject of my sermon?

In addition to scenery and props, what about costuming? Do you need to be in costume if you are doing a first-person characterization? Does it add to the story if you are in period costume? There is considerable debate about this issue. Basically, there are two approaches to this issue.

Costuming

Congregations with an active drama program have a wealth of costuming options. A simple biblical garb can suffice. If you are going to use some kind of costuming, please recognize that your presentation may no longer seem to be a sermon. Simplicity of costume can be quite effective. As a rule of thumb, anything that detracts from your presentation of the gospel is unneeded and unnecessary. On the other hand, some members of your congregation may have degrees in fashion design. The creation of costuming can be a marvelous outlet for someone who desires to contribute to the church in a meaningful way. In addition, theater companies in most communities might be willing to lend costumes or lend a hand with such a task. This can be another avenue of outreach into your community. Every year, I have conducted an Advent service called "Hanging of the Greens." In this service, we decorate the sanctuary for Christmas. One year, we focused several worship services on the gifts of the Magi. One of the ladies in the church did an amazing amount of research into fabric and design to create costuming that would befit the Magi and their social and economic status, as well as reflect the cultural influences of their day. As three men came down the aisle, it was quite impressive to watch and learn. I am not suggesting that costuming should always go to such lengths, but remember that effective period costumes can enhance the presentation of a narrative sermon.

STORYTELLER GARB

Most storytellers that I know do not use costuming. If they frequently depict a certain character, though, they may create an appropriate costume for that character. Otherwise, they don't feel that a costume is necessary. Why? Because they know that a story can stand on its own without the aid of anything else. Preachers who do first-person narrative sermons eventually learn that the story can carry the day. The closer you get to looking like you are on stage, the more your sermon becomes a performance and less inspirational or instructive. A good storyteller can merely lean in toward an audience, speak an opening line, and then be off and running. Even if the crowd is not expecting a narrative approach, they catch on quickly. In storytelling, the story is what matters, not the garb. At its most basic, storyteller garb is not a costume at all; it merely allows the story to take center stage while you become part of the background.

EPILOGUE

However you choose to use narrative preaching, remember that a worship experience should fully involve the senses of the worshiper. We have designed most of our church sanctuaries to be visually pleasing or to create a desired affect or mood. In narrative preaching, the surroundings may help to tell the story, but a true storyteller is ready to speak anyplace, anytime, with any group, and in any setting. You may want to use props and costumes to create visual variety to your preaching, even as you create diversity in your preaching styles.

Preaching the story should be foremost in your mind. As God leads you into this exciting and expanding area of ministry, keep focused on his story. It is not so much about the things that surround you. At the heart of it all, narrative preaching is just telling how God deals with us. If you love to tell that story and if it will indeed be your "theme in glory," then I encourage you to keep on learning new ways to tell the old, old story of Jesus and his love. Keep on preaching the story.

BIBLIOGRAPHY

Anderson, Bernhard W. *Out of the Depths: The Psalms Speak to Us Today.* Philadelphia: Westminster, 1974.

Barclay, William. *Introduction to the First Three Gospels.* Philadelphia: Westminster, 1975.

Barker, Joel. *The Business of Paradigms.* 2nd ed. VHS. St. Paul, MN: Star Thrower Distribution, 1990.

Barna, George. *Baby Busters: The Disillusioned Generation.* Chicago: Northfield Publishing, 1994.

Bewer, Julius A. *The Literature of the Old Testament.* Rev. ed. New York: Columbia University Press, 1933.

Bishop, Jennie. *The Squire and the Scroll.* Anderson, IN: Warner Press, 2004.

———. *The Princess and the Kiss.* Anderson, IN: Warner Press, 1999.

Breneman, Bren, and Lucille N. Breneman. *Once upon a Time: A Storytelling Handbook.* Chicago: Nelson-Hall, 1983.

Buttrick, David. "On Doing Homiletics Today." In *Intersections: Post-Critical Studies in Preaching,* edited by Richard L. Eslinger, 88–104. Grand Rapids, MI: Eerdmans, 1994.

Cicero. *On the Orator,* book 1. In *Rhetorical Treatises,* vol. 3, *De oratore, Books 1–2,* translated by E. W. Sutton. Loeb Classical Library 348. Cambridge, MA: Harvard University Press, 1942.

Craddock, Fred. *As One without Authority.* Enid, OK: Phillips University Press, 1974.

Earle, Ralph. *Beacon Bible Commentary: Acts.* Kansas City, KS: Beacon Hill, 1965.

Eslinger, Richard L. *Narrative and Imagination: Preaching the Worlds that Shape Us.* Minneapolis: Fortress, 1995.

Green, Joel. B. "The (Re-)Turn to Narrative." In Green and Pasquarello, *Narrative Reading, Narrative Preaching,* 11–36.

Green, Joel B., and Michael Pasquarello III, eds. *Narrative Reading, Narrative Preaching: Reuniting New Testament Interpretation and Proclamation.* Grand Rapids, MI: Baker Academic, 2003.

Grossman, Lev. "Blogs Have Their Day." *Time,* December 27, 2004, 109.

Hagan, Uta, with Haskel Frankel. *Respect for Acting.* New York: Macmillan, 1973.

Hybels, Bill, Stuart Briscoe, and Haddon Robinson. *Mastering Contemporary Preaching.* Portland, OR: Multnomah, 1989.

Laughlin, Gerard. *Telling God's Story: Bible, Church, and Narrative Theology.* New York: Cambridge University Press, 1996.

BIBLIOGRAPHY

Livo, Norma J., and Sandra A. Reitz. *Storytelling: Process and Practice.* Littleton, CO: Libraries Unlimited, 1986.

Loscalzo, Craig A. "Rhetoric." In *Concise Encyclopedia of Preaching,* edited by William H. Willimon and Richard Lischer, 409–16. Louisville: Westminster John Knox, 1995.

Lowry, Eugene L. *The Homiletical Plot: The Sermon as Narrative Art.* Atlanta: John Knox, 1980.

———. *The Sermon: Dancing on the Edge of Mystery.* Nashville: Abingdon, 1997.

Lucas, Jerry. *Learning How to Learn.* Dallas: Lucas Educational Systems, 2001.

———. *His Word—The Book of Mark.* Atlanta: Jerry Lucas, 1981.

Massey, James Earl. *The Responsible Pulpit.* Anderson, IN: Warner Press, 1974.

Meyer, Eric. "The Six Steps of Uta Hagen." EricMeyer.net. http://www.ericmeyer.net/actor/sixsteps.html (accessed March 9, 2006).

Nelson, Roy Paul. *The Design of Advertising.* 4th ed. Dubuque, IA: Wm. C. Brown, 1977.

Robinson, Haddon W. *Biblical Preaching: The Development and Delivery of Expository Messages.* Grand Rapids, MI: Baker Book House, 1980.

Seventh-Day Adventists. *Church Manual.* Silver Spring, MD: General Conference of Seventh-Day Adventists, 2006. http://www.adventist.org/beliefs/church_manual/.

Stanislovski, Constantin. *Creating a Role.* Translated by Elizabeth Reynolds Hapgood. New York: Theater Arts Books, 1961.

Turner, Philip Williams. *Christ in the Concrete City: A Play for a Cast of Four Men and Two Women.* London: SPCK, for the Religious Drama Society of Great Britain, 1960. Rev. ed., Quincy, MA: Baker's Plays, 1983.

Walsh, John. *The Art of Storytelling.* Chicago: Moody Publishers, 2003.

Warren, Rick. *The Purpose-Driven Life.* Grand Rapids, MI: Zondervan, 2002.

Weinreich, Beatrice Silverman, ed. *Yiddish Folktales.* Translated by Leonard Wolf. New York: Pantheon Books, 1988.

Wilson, Paul Scott. *The Practice of Preaching.* Nashville: Abingdon, 1995.

Willimon, William H. "Preaching the Letters as Narrative." In Green and Pasquarello, *Narrative Reading, Narrative Preaching, 107–17.*